How To Use This Study Guide

This 15-lesson study guide corresponds to *"Easter — The Rest of the Story"* *With Rick Renner* (**Renner TV**). Each lesson in this study guide covers a topic that is addressed during the program series, with questions and references supplied to draw you deeper into your own private study of the Scriptures on this subject.

To derive the most benefit from this study guide, consider the following:

First, watch or listen to the program prior to working through the corresponding lesson in this guide. (Programs can also be viewed at **renner.org** by clicking on the Media/Archives links or on our Renner Ministries YouTube channel.)

Second, take the time to look up the scriptures included in each lesson. Prayerfully consider their application to your own life.

Third, use a journal or notebook to make note of your answers to each lesson's Study Questions and Practical Application challenges.

Fourth, invest specific time in prayer and in the Word of God to consult with the Holy Spirit. Write down the scriptures or insights He reveals to you.

Finally, take action! Whatever the Lord tells you to do according to His Word, do it.

For added insights on this subject, it is recommended that you obtain Rick Renner's book *Easter — The Rest of the Story.* You may also select from Rick's other available resources by placing your order at **renner.org** or by calling 1-800-742-5593.

TOPIC

Agony of the Soul and Divine Assistance

SCRIPTURES

1. **Luke 22:44** — And being in an agony he prayed more earnestly: and his sweat was as it were great drops of blood falling down to the ground.

2. **Luke 22:42,43** — Saying, Father, if thou be willing, remove this cup from me: nevertheless not my will, but thine, be done. And there appeared an angel unto him from heaven, strengthening him.

3. **Mark 14:42** — Rise up, let us go; lo, he that betrayeth me is at hand.

GREEK WORDS

1. "agony" (*agonidzo*) — depicts a struggle, a fight, great exertion, or great effort; used in the New Testament to convey the ideas of anguish, pain, distress, and conflict, and it is where we get the English word agony; the word *agonidzo* comes from the word *agon*, a Greek word that depicted the athletic conflicts and competitions that were so strenuous in the ancient world

2. "earnestly" (*ektenes*) — to be extended or to be stretched out

3. "sweat" (*idros*)— sweaty sweat

4. "drops" (*thrombos*)— a medical word that points to blood that is unusually thickly clotted

5. "strengthening" *(ischuos)* — to impart strength, to empower someone, to fill a person with heartiness, or to give someone a renewed vitality; although one may feel exhausted and depleted, he suddenly gets a blast of energy so robust that he is instantly recharged and ready to get up, get with it, and get going again

A Note From Rick Renner

I am on a personal Quest to see a "revival of the Bible" so people can establish their lives on a firm foundation that will stand strong and endure the test as end-time storm winds begin to intensify.

In order to experience a revival of the Bible in your personal life, it is important to take time each day to read, receive, and apply its truths to your life. James tells us that if we will continue in the perfect law of liberty — refusing to be forgetful hearers, but determined to be doers — we will be blessed in our ways. As you watch or listen to the programs in this series and work through this corresponding study guide, I trust you will search the Scriptures and allow the Holy Spirit to help you hear something new from God's Word that applies specifically to your life. I encourage you to be a doer of the Word He reveals to you. Whatever the cost, I assure you — it will be worth it.

> Thy words were found, and I did eat them;
> and thy word was unto me the joy and rejoicing of mine heart:
> for I am called by thy name, O Lord God of hosts.
> — Jeremiah 15:16

Your brother and friend in Jesus Christ,

Rick Renner

Easter — The Rest of the Story

Copyright © 2025 by Rick Renner
1814 W. Tacoma St.
Broken Arrow, OK 74012-1406

Published by Rick Renner Ministries
www.renner.org

ISBN 13: 978-1-6675-1191-7

eBook ISBN 13: 978-1-6675-1192-4

SYNOPSIS

The 15 lessons in this study titled *Easter — The Rest of the Story* will focus on the following topics:

- Agony of the Soul and Divine Assistance
- How Many Soldiers Did It Take To Arrest One Man?
- The Judas Kiss
- Peter's Mess and the Naked Boy in the Garden of Gethsemane
- Spitting in Jesus' Face and Playing Games With Jesus
- Pilate Looks for a Loophole
- Herod Finally Meets Jesus
- The Horror of a Roman Scourging
- Golgotha — 'The Place of the Skull'
- 'IT IS FINISHED!'
- Buried and Sealed
- 'Behold, He Is Risen!'
- Eyewitnesses of Jesus' Resurrection
- What Has Jesus Been Doing for the Last 2,000 Years?
- Copy Every Stroke of the Master and Walk in the Footprints of Jesus!

When people visit the city of Jerusalem, there are several sites they want to see. These include the Church of the Holy Sepulcher, which is the site that is traditionally believed to be where Jesus was crucified and the tomb where He was buried and then raised from the dead. There is also the Western Wall, or "Wailing Wall," and the Garden tomb (also known as Gordon's Calvary), which is another possible location of Jesus' burial and resurrection. Another site people often want to visit is the Garden of Gethsemane, which is the place we will explore extensively in this first lesson.

The emphasis of this lesson:

The Garden of Gethsemane is a sacred place spoken of in all four gospels where Jesus agonized in prayer and received supernatural strength from the Father to endure the Roman scourge, the crucifixion, and the

grave. That same divine assistance is available to you when you ask God for help.

The Garden of Gethsemane

On the lower slopes of the Mount of Olives in Jerusalem there is an ancient garden where olive trees were once grown in large numbers, and it was also where olives were crushed and pressed to produce olive oil. Also scattered on the slopes of the Mount of Olives are ancient graves, where wealthier Jews were buried at the time of Jesus.

In this ancient olive grove called the Garden of Gethsemane, behind an ornamented fence, are the gnarled trunks of eight massive olive trees that could possibly date to the time of Jesus. To see if these ancient trees in Gethsemane were around in Christ's day, scientists conducted radiocarbon-dating testing on some of the roots, and the results indeed indicated that some of the roots could possibly be 2,000 years old.

That means the massive olive trees standing there today could actually be descendants of those that were in the garden at the time of Christ. If this is true, then it's possible that some of those trees were there at the time of Jesus' agony and are silent witnesses to the events that occurred in the garden the night He was betrayed.

Indeed, many significant events in the life of Jesus took place in the Garden of Gethsemane, and it is for this reason that Christians from all over the world have been making pilgrimages to that garden for 2,000 years.

Today most visitors enter the Garden of Gethsemane through an ancient stone gate, and then they meander onward on a path that encircles the eight age-old olive trees that can still be seen there. Finally, as they walk around that fenced-off area, they eventually make their way to the entrance of the Church of All Nations, a building that was constructed on the ruins of a Byzantine basilica that was originally erected on that site to commemorate the events that took place with Jesus in the Garden of Gethsemane.

It was in 1920 that archeologists discovered the Fourth-Century foundation of this basilica along with fragments of magnificent mosaics. In response, they began to work in conjunction with architects to construct the Church of All Nations, which was officially consecrated in April 1924. It is surrounded by an iron fence that looks like a crown of thorns, and inside this church is an exposed outcropping of rock where it is believed Christ prayed His final night in the Gethsemane.

That exposed outcropping is a rock where tradition says Jesus agonizingly prayed in His last hours, and there is every reason to believe that large protruding stone really is the place where Jesus prayed and sweat large drops of blood during his time of prayer there.

There Is Also a Grotto in Gethsemane

There is another very important place that most tourists don't know about when they visit Gethsemane. They are so focused on seeing the ancient, gnarled olive trees and the stone outcropping where Jesus prayed that they completely miss the grotto — or cave — located just across the street from the Garden of Gethsemane.

Down several flights of stone steps, and at the end of a narrow pathway lined with stone walls on each side, is an entrance that leads to an underground grotto that early Christian writers said Jesus regularly used to assemble with his disciples when they visited the Garden of Gethsemane.

Because this grotto was underground, it was an ideal place to gather because it provided shelter from inclement weather, and it was a quiet, isolated space. Based on early Christian tradition, Jesus regularly gathered in that grotto in Gethsemane with his disciples to rest and pray when they were in Jerusalem.

In fact, it was such a regular meeting place for Jesus and His disciples that when Judas Iscariot led the cohort of Roman soldiers and the temple police to arrest Jesus, he knew that he would find Jesus and His followers in that grotto because he had retreated there with Jesus and the other apostles so frequently.

But on the night Jesus was betrayed and arrested, He felt the need to pray, so He left all but three of His disciples alone in the grotto and went a short distance from them to pray. This place is the famous outcropping of rock that people visit today in the Church of All Nations in Jerusalem. Thus, the Grotto of Gethsemane was a regular gathering place for Jesus and His disciples.

On the Night He Was Betrayed, Jesus Pulled Away and Prayed

According to the New Testament, after Jesus finished serving Communion to His disciples in the upper room, He went to the Garden of Gethsemane with them. Knowing that the Roman scourge, the Cross, and the grave were coming, He felt an urgency to spend time in intercession so He might gain the strength needed to face what lay before Him.

As He was gathered with 11 of His disciples inside the grotto, Jesus requested that Peter, James, and John come apart with Him to pray. Although He rarely needed His friends' assistance, in this unprecedented and intense moment, Jesus felt a need to have His three closest disciples pray with Him. Leaving eight disciples in the cave, Jesus and His inner circle of three made their way to the outcropping stone where He began to agonize in prayer.

Sadly, instead of faithfully praying at the time Jesus desperately needed their support, the three disciples kept falling asleep. But, thankfully, God the Father provided supernatural assistance for Jesus, which is exactly what He will do for you when you're going through difficult times. If you feel like your closest friends have abandoned you, you are not alone. God is with you and will give you the strength you need to make it through even your toughest hours.

Please note that the events that occurred in the Garden of Gethsemane are so crucial to the story of Jesus' passion that elements of what took place are recorded in all four gospels: Matthew 26; Mark 14; Luke 22; and John 18.

The 'Agony' Jesus Faced Was Intense

The mental, emotional, and spiritual battle Jesus experienced that final night in the Garden of Gethsemane was overwhelming. Here are some details recorded by the physician Luke that are found only in his gospel:

> **And being in an agony he prayed more earnestly: and his sweat was as it were great drops of blood falling down to the ground.**
> **— Luke 22:44**

A closer look at the original Greek text of this verse gives us a better understanding of what Jesus was experiencing during His time of intense intercession. First, notice the word "agony." It is the Greek word *agonidzo*, which depicts *a struggle, a fight, great exertion, or great effort*. It is used in the New Testament to convey the ideas of *anguish, pain, distress*, and *conflict*, and it is where we get the English word *agony*.

The word *agonidzo* comes from the word *agon*, a Greek term that depicted the athletic conflicts and competitions that were so strenuous in the ancient world. The use of this word lets us know that in this particular moment, Jesus was thrown into the fight of His life. It was a time of tremendous *anguish, pain*, and *agony*.

The Holy Spirit intentionally used this word *agonidzo* in these verses to help us understand the battle that Jesus experienced in the Garden of Gethsemane on the night of His betrayal, and it tells us that Jesus was thrown into a great struggle or an intense fight that night.

Christ Cried Out to the Father for Help

Knowing all that was before Him, Jesus cried out to the Father again and again...

> **Saying, Father, if thou be willing, remove this cup from me: nevertheless not my will, but thine, be done.**
> — Luke 22:42

In His heart, Jesus knew what He had to do. He knew He would be beaten and spit on by the Jewish leaders and that He would receive the horrific Roman scourge, which meant being lacerated across His back and His body with numerous stripes. Likewise, He knew that His hands and feet would be nailed to the Cross, and that He would experience death and descend into hell for three days.

The spiritual pressure that bore down upon Jesus' soul was so overwhelming that the Bible says it was *agonidzo*, or it was *an agonizing event*. In fact, the fight was so strenuous that it involved all of Jesus' Spirit, soul, and body. Indeed, he was in the greatest fight He had ever known up to that moment, and when He most needed the prayers of His friends, they were sleeping on the job.

How intense were Jesus' prayers? Luke 22:44 says, "And being in an agony he [Jesus] prayed more earnestly...." Jesus' intense level of agony is depicted in the word "earnestly," which is translated from the Greek word *ektenes*, meaning *to be extended* or *to be stretched out*.

A person in this kind of agony might drop to the ground, writhing in pain, rolling this way and that way on the ground. This word presents the picture of a person who is pushed to the limit and can't be stretched much more. He is on the brink of all he can possibly endure. That is where Jesus was in that moment.

The Internal Anguish Was So Intense, Jesus Sweat 'Drops of Blood'

Luke 22:44 goes on to tell us Jesus' emotional state was so intense that "…his sweat was as it were great drops of blood falling down to the ground." The word "sweat" here describes *sweaty sweat*, and the Greek word for "drops" is a medical word that points to *blood that is unusually thickly clotted*.

The definitions of these two words means that the phrase "sweat great drops of blood" describes the Greek term *hematidrosis*, a real medical condition that only occurs in individuals who are in a highly emotional state, which takes place very rarely.

In this medical condition, because the mind is under such great mental and emotional pressure, it sends signals of stress throughout the human body, and these signals are so strong that the body reacts as if it is under actual physical pressure.

As a result of this perceived pressure, the first and second layer of skin separate, causing a vacuum to form between them and fill with thickly clotted blood. That blood then seeps from this vacuum and oozes through the pores of the skin. Once the blood seeps through the pores of the skin, it mingles with the sufferer's sweat that is pouring from his body as a result of his intense struggle.

In the end, the oozing blood and sweat mingle together in droplets, which flow down the victim's face and body. It is this state of *hematidrosis* that Jesus experienced in the Garden of Gethsemane the night of His betrayal.

The Holy Spirit included these details about Jesus' sweating blood to alert us to the fact that this was the most intense spiritual combat He had ever endured up to this time. As He faced the multiple trials, the scourging, the crown of thorns, the crucifixion, and three days in hell, Jesus was in the fight for His life — and the battle of the ages.

God Infused Jesus With Supernatural Strength

Where were Jesus' disciples when He needed them most? What did they do when He asked them to pray with Him for one hour? They were sleeping on the job. But in their dereliction of duty, God the Father personally provided supernatural assistance for Jesus in another way. The Bible says:

> **And there appeared an angel unto him from heaven, strengthening him.**
> — Luke 22:43

The word "strengthening" in this verse is the Greek word *enischuo*, a compound of the words *en* and *ischuos*. The word *en* means *in*, as in to put something into something, and the word *ischuos* is the word for *might*. When these two words are compounded to form *enischuo* — translated here as "strengthening" — it means *to put might or strength into something*. That is exactly what happened to Jesus when He was in agony in Gethsemane. When His friends abandoned Him, God the Father sent an angel from Heaven that filled Jesus with *might*!

This word "strengthening" means *to impart strength*, *to empower someone*, *to fill a person with heartiness*, or *to give someone a renewed vitality*. Although one may feel exhausted and depleted, when he is strengthened by God, he suddenly gets a blast of energy so robust that he is instantly recharged and ready to get up, get with it, and get going again.

When the angel appeared and strengthened Jesus, He was instantly recharged and filled with vitality, enabling Him to get up, get with it, and get going. That is what we find Jesus doing in Mark 14:42. After being filled with might by the angel, Jesus got up, went to His disciples who were sleeping, and said, "Rise up, let us go; lo, he that betrayeth me is at hand." He then returned to the grotto in Gethsemane and rejoined the other eight disciples

If You're Going Through Great Difficulty, Jesus Knows How You Feel and Wants To Help

Have you ever been in a situation that caused you such intense agony that you felt the need for help from your friends, but you found that they couldn't be counted on? Did you find them "sleeping on the job" when you felt a deep need for their help and support? If so, don't be upset with them. They probably just don't have the ability to comprehend what you are going through.

Maybe you've never sweat blood like Jesus did, but it is likely that you have struggled in your soul at one time or another because of problems with your marriage, your children, your relationships, your ministry, your health, your finances, or due to a concern for the well-being of loved ones.

If you've experienced these kinds of stressful situations, then you know that continuous pressure is hard to deal with — especially if you have no one to lean on for strength, encouragement, and help in that moment. If you are experiencing one of those times right now, Jesus understands because He faced the same situation in the Garden of Gethsemane. He was under such intense pressure that He sweat drops of blood, and He will help you if you reach out to Him and ask for it.

So regardless of the battle or situation you're facing in life right now, just as God provided supernatural strength for Jesus, He will provide divine assistance for you too. The same divine help He provided for Christ in the Garden of Gethsemane is what He will also provide for you. He may send an angel, another unexpected person who understands and wants to help, or He may refill you with the Holy Spirit in a way that super-charges you to face and overcome that difficult moment.

In our next lesson, we will learn about the actual number of soldiers that came into the Garden of Gethsemane to arrest Jesus and why they carried such deadly weapons with them.

STUDY QUESTIONS

Study to shew thyself approved unto God, a workman that needeth not to be ashamed, rightly dividing the word of truth.
— 2 Timothy 2:15

1. The Garden of Gethsemane is a sacred place where Jesus agonized in prayer and received the strength He would need to fulfill the Father's will and become the Lamb of God, as had been prophesied in Scripture. What new insights did you learn about this remarkable place?

2. When the disciples fell asleep and failed to pray with Jesus, God Himself provided supernatural strength that carried Jesus through all the cruelty He would suffer. If you feel like those closest to you have abandoned

you, God is still with you! And He promises to give you all the strength you need to make it through. Read Isaiah 40:29-31 (*AMPC*), Second Corinthians 12:9 and 10 (*AMPC*), and Philippians 4:13 (*AMPC*). Take time to identify and meditate on the promises found in these verses.

PRACTICAL APPLICATION

But be ye doers of the word, and not hearers only,
deceiving your own selves.
— James 1:22

1. As Jesus wrestled in prayer, "…his sweat was as it were great drops of blood falling down to the ground" (Luke 22:44). Prior to this lesson, what did you understand this verse to mean? How does the knowledge that this is a real medical condition (*hematidrosis*) reframe your image of Jesus praying in the garden?

2. When you really stop to think of the intense weight of all that Jesus was about to face (the scourge, the Cross, the grave, and more), to redeem you and all mankind, how does it expand and change your perception of what He was going through in the Garden of Gethsemane?

LESSON 2

TOPIC

How Many Soldiers Did It Take To Arrest One Man?

SCRIPTURES

1. **John 21:25** — And there are also many other things which Jesus did, the which, if they should be written every one, I suppose that even the world itself could not contain the books that should be written. Amen.

2. **John 18:3** — Judas then, having received a band of men and officers from the chief priests and Pharisees, cometh thither with lanterns and torches and weapons.

3. **Mark 14:43** — And immediately, while he yet spake, cometh Judas, one of the twelve, and with him a great multitude with swords and staves....

GREEK WORDS

1. "a band of men" (*speira*) — a Roman cohort; somewhere between 300 to 600 well-trained soldiers who were equipped with the finest weaponry of the day
2. "officers" (*huperetas*)— temple police who worked for the chief priests and Pharisees on the temple grounds
3. "lanterns"(*phanos*) — a bright and shining light; a light to "light up" a dark room so you can see things better; pictures a light that was the equivalent of a First-Century flashlight that produced a beam so brilliant it could penetrate darkened areas and reveal things hidden in darkness
4. "torches" (*lampas*)— a long-burning oil lamp; these were oil-based, had a long wick, and could burn all night, if necessary
5. "weapons" (*hoplon*) — the full weaponry of a Roman soldier — a belt, a breastplate, shoes, an oblong shield, a helmet, a sword, and a lance
6. "sword" (*machaira*) — a deadly type of sword used for stabbing someone at close range
7. "stave" (*zhulos*)— a thick, heavy stick made of wood; a heavy-duty, dangerous, hard-hitting club intended to beat someone

SYNOPSIS

On the night Jesus was betrayed, Judas Iscariot knew where the Lord would be. The Bible says, "And Judas, who betrayed Him, also knew the place; for Jesus often met there with His disciples" (John 18:2 *NKJV*).

The place where Jesus often retreated with His disciples was the Garden of Gethsemane, and that is where Judas led a group of temple police guards and a band of men who had been assigned to go and arrest Jesus. But just how many soldiers were in that band? And why were they armed with lanterns, torches, and weapons? Answers to these and other questions will be discovered in this lesson.

The emphasis of this lesson:

When Judas led the soldiers and officers to capture Jesus, he came with a mob of hundreds of men who were equipped with bright lights and long-lasting oil lamps to search for Jesus until He was found. Jesus' power was legendary, even in His day, which is why the soldiers were also armed with deadly weapons and prepared to take Him by force if needed.

A Brief Review of Lesson 1

In our first lesson, we learned several things about the Garden of Gethsemane. It is located on the lower slopes of the Mount of Olives near Jerusalem and surrounded by a stone fence. Shortly after entering the gate, you will find yourself in the interior courtyard where there are eight massive ancient olive trees, some of which date to the time of Jesus.

Recent carbon dating tests conducted on the roots of the trees confirmed that several of them are 2,000 years old, which means some of these trees could very well be silent witnesses to the agony Jesus suffered in Gethsemane the night He was betrayed.

If you were to walk a bit farther into the garden, you would eventually enter the Church of All Nations. It was constructed in the early 1920s after archaeologists discovered the ruins of the foundation of a Fourth-Century Byzantine basilica that was originally built to commemorate the events that took place with Jesus in Gethsemane.

We also noted that the centerpiece inside the Church of All Nations is an exposed outcropping of rock where tradition says Jesus agonizingly prayed in His last hours and sweat great drops of blood. This is one of the most visited sites in Jerusalem.

When you exit the church, leaving the central gate of the Garden of Gethsemane, and meander back through the courtyard, there is another gate just across the street. If you follow the steps down to a lower level, through a long rock passageway, you'll find a cave that is called the Grotto of Gethsemane. Although most people have never heard of it, it is the place where most of the events in the Garden of Gethsemane occurred.

In fact, it was in that very grotto, or cave, that Jesus and His disciples would regularly assemble to rest and pray. It was a sacred space where they could retreat and have safe shelter from all kinds of inclement weather. It was to this grotto that Judas took the temple police and the band of soldiers the night Jesus was arrested.

The 'Grotto' in Gethsemane has Been Virtually Unchanged Since Jesus' Day

On the night of His betrayal, when Jesus was finished praying in the Garden of Gethsemane, He returned with Peter, James, and John to the grotto where the other eight disciples remained while He was praying. As we noted, that grotto is where many events played out in the final hours of Christ's life before He was arrested.

Although this cave was converted into a chapel in the Fourth Century, today the interior has been basically unchanged since the time of Jesus — with the exception that there is now an altar, candles, and several wooden chairs for worshipers to use while they stop to pray and seek God.

There are also paintings on the walls of the cave, including one that depicts the kiss of betrayal that Judas gave to Jesus the night that he betrayed Christ, as well as a depiction of Jesus' appearance after His resurrection. Furthermore, on the walls of this grotto is an ancient inscription still visible today which states: "Christ, the Savior, frequented this place with His apostles."

It was this frequented place that Jesus and His disciples went to on the night He was betrayed. Judas Iscariot was very familiar with this grotto in Gethsemane, which is why he went there that fateful night, accompanied by religious leaders, Roman soldiers, and temple police.

Jesus Was a Legend in His Own Day

When you think about the number of soldiers and temple police officers that came to capture Christ and bring Him into custody, what picture comes to mind? Because it has been misrepresented in various movies, most people tend to imagine it was Judas and a handful of soldiers who showed up. But the fact is that it was a massive mob that came to arrest Jesus that night.

Keep in mind that Jesus' power was legendary. In fact, the Bible states He was so renowned that even Herod Antipas had wanted to meet Him for a long time (*see* Luke 23:8).

- Jesus healed the sick.
- Jesus cast out demons.
- Jesus raised the dead.
- Jesus walked on water.
- Jesus changed water into wine.
- Jesus multiplied loaves and fishes.

Indeed, the power of Jesus was already legendary, even during the three and a half years of His earthly ministry. The apostle John made a statement about Jesus' creative power in the closing remarks of his gospel, telling us:

> **And there are also many other things which Jesus did, the which, if they should be written every one, I suppose that even the world itself could not contain the books that should be written. Amen.**
>
> **— John 21:25**

Religious leaders had tried to capture Jesus on numerous occasions, but each time, He miraculously slipped away from them. You can read about this in Luke 4:30; John 7:30; John 8:59; and John 10:39. The fact that Jesus had supernaturally slipped out of their hands on other occasions caused the religious leaders to fear He might slip away from them again.

That is why Judas Iscariot led a massive group of Roman soldiers and temple police to arrest Jesus that night in the Grotto of Gethsemane. It was far too many soldiers to capture just one individual — unless that individual was the Son of God.

Again, Judas knew exactly where to find Jesus. He knew that the armed mob with him could find Jesus in the Grotto of Gethsemane because he had been there often with Jesus and the other disciples.

How Many Roman Soldiers and Temple Police Came With Judas To Arrest Jesus?

To get an understanding of how many men were with Judas the night of Jesus' arrest, we turn to John 18:3, which says, "Judas then, having received a band of men and officers from the chief priests and Pharisees, cometh thither with lanterns and torches and weapons."

The "band of men" with Judas was made up of Roman soldiers who were stationed at the Tower of Antonia, a large military post for the Romans connected to the Temple Mount. This structure had been built by King Herod the Great, and he named it after Mark Antony who was his friend. The Tower of Antonia housed many Roman soldiers, and they usually resided inside the inner courtyard. The reason they were stationed there is because even in the First Century, the Temple Mount was a hot spot, and the soldiers were there to make sure there were no disruptions or riots that took place.

John 18:3 says Judas brought "a band of men." This phrase is a translation of the Greek word *speira*, which describes *a military cohort* — somewhere between 300 to 600 well-trained Roman soldiers who were equipped with the finest weaponry of the day. That said, we see that Judas came with a minimum of 300 — possibly as many as 600 — soldiers armed to the max to arrest Jesus.

Along with these soldiers was a number of "officers" (*see* John 18:3). In Greek, the word "officers" describes *temple police* who worked for the chief priests and Pharisees on the temple grounds. Once a religious verdict was issued from the Jewish court, it was the responsibility of these "temple police" to carry out the judgments. This was a brutal, religious, armed force that reported to the chief priests, the Pharisees, and the Sanhedrin, and they worked in conjunction with the Roman cohort stationed at the Tower of Antonia to keep the peace on the Temple Mount.

So when John 18:3 says "officers" came to arrest Jesus, this refers to the fearsome "temple police" who accompanied "a band of men" — a cohort of 300 to 600 Roman soldiers. Thus, at a minimum, there were 300 soldiers — possibly up to 600 soldiers — plus temple police that accompanied Judas. More than likely, the overall number of Roman soldiers and temple police exceeded 600.

That night, the hillside where the Garden of Gethsemane is located was swarming with hundreds of Roman soldiers and highly trained militia from the Temple Mount. Such a large number of troops sent to arrest one man shows how panicked the religious leaders were about Jesus escaping them again.

All Four Gospels Confirm
a 'Great Multitude' Accompanied Judas

What is interesting is that all four gospel writers — Matthew, Mark, Luke, and John — all verify that the number of soldiers and officers that came to arrest Jesus in the Garden of Gethsemane was massive.

Matthew 26:47 states:

> …Judas, one of the twelve, came, and with him *a great multitude* with swords and staves, from the chief priests and elders of the people.

The words "a great multitude" in Greek describe *a huge or massive multitude* of soldiers.

Mark 14:43 reports:

> And immediately, while he yet spake, cometh Judas, one of the twelve, and with him *a great multitude* with swords and staves, from the chief priests and the scribes and the elders.

Once again, the phrase "a great multitude" in the original Greek language emphatically and unquestionably describes *a massive crowd* that came to arrest Jesus.

Luke 22:47 says:

> And while he [Jesus] yet spake, behold *a multitude*, and he that was called Judas, one of the twelve, went before them, and drew near unto Jesus to kiss him.

The word "multitude" in this verse is the same Greek word used in Mark's gospel, and it describes *an enormous crowd* that accompanied Judas.

We've seen that John wrote:

> Judas then, having received a band of men and officers from the chief priests and Pharisees, cometh thither with lanterns and torches and weapons.
> — John 18:3

Again, the phrase "a band of men" is translated from the Greek word *speira*, which describes *a Roman cohort* — somewhere between 300 to 600 well-trained soldiers who were equipped with the finest weaponry of the day.

Therefore, it is very likely that the combined number of Roman soldiers and temple police exceeded 600 men. Rather than coming with a handful of soldiers, as you may have imagined, Judas came with a small army. He may have warned them that Jesus and His disciples might put up a fight, or it is possible that the chief priests and religious leaders were nervous that Jesus might release divine power to resist them. Thus, they came ready for a fight.

The Mob Came With 'Lanterns and Torches'

Now that you have a more accurate picture of the hundreds of soldiers and temple police that came to arrest Jesus, it is also important to notice what they brought with them. Looking again at John 18:3, we read, "Judas then, having received a band of men and officers from the chief priests and Pharisees, cometh thither with *lanterns and torches* and weapons."

First, it says they carried "lanterns and torches." This tells us that the soldiers were ready to intensely hunt and search for Jesus everywhere, for as long as necessary, until they found Him. Could it be that Judas or those with Him thought that Jesus would hide? A fact that you may not know is that the Garden of Gethsemane was filled with many caves in which Jesus could have hidden.

But that would not be what Jesus chose to do. This time, He would willingly surrender Himself to the authorities. He knew it was the will of the Father and the appointed time for Him — the Lamb of God — to sacrifice His life on the altar of the Cross to save everyone that would believe in Him.

Of course, the mob of militia that accompanied Judas didn't know what Jesus and His disciples would do, so they came armed to the max, carrying "lanterns" and "torches." The word "lanterns" here describes *a bright and shining light* or *a light to "light up" a dark room so you can see things better*. It pictures a light that was the equivalent of a first-century flashlight that produced a beam so brilliant that it could penetrate darkened areas and reveal things that were hidden.

Along with lanterns, they also brought *torches*. Unlike "lanterns" that were short-lived, these "torches" were long-lasting. In Greek, the word for "torches" describes *a long-burning oil lamp*. These were oil-based, had a long wick, and could burn all night, if necessary. Hence, the Roman soldiers and temple police carried enough bright shining lights and long-burning oil lamps to light up the whole hillside so they could hunt for Jesus all night long.

The Soldiers Were Armed for a Fight

Something else that the Bible specifically tells us about this massive group of soldiers and temple police is that they came with *weapons* (*see* John 18:3). In Greek, the word "weapons" is *hoplon*, which describes *the full weaponry of a Roman soldier — a belt, breastplate, shoes, oblong shield, a helmet, a sword, and a lance.* These 300 to 600 soldiers were armed for a confrontation!

Mark's gospel confirms John's account, telling us that along with Judas, there came "…a great multitude with *swords* and *staves*…" (Mark 14:43). The word "sword" here describes *a deadly type of sword used for stabbing someone at close range.* Does this mean the temple police were ready to stab and draw blood that night? It is certainly possible.

Scripture says the mob was also armed with "staves," which are *thick, heavy sticks made of wood* or *heavy-duty, hard-hitting clubs* that were dangerous and intended for beating someone. Clearly, regardless of the intentions of the soldiers and temple police, they were prepared to beat down any resistance and take Jesus into custody.

How Well Did Judas Know Jesus?

Remember, the stories of Jesus' miracles were already legendary, and Judas Iscariot knew of Jesus' power and had seen its miraculous abilities. Surprisingly, what Judas didn't realize, even after walking side by side with Jesus in ministry for more than three years, was that Jesus wasn't going to fight. On that night, no one had to forcibly take Him — because the battle was over.

Jesus had already won the victory over His flesh when He wrestled in prayer earlier in the Garden of Gethsemane. He had known for quite some time that it was the Father's will for Him to die on the Cross as the Lamb of God and, ultimately, be resurrected from the dead, so He willingly surrendered and entrusted Himself into the hands of the Father.

But Judas' actions should really make us question just how well he knew Jesus. When Jesus saw Judas with hundreds upon hundreds of soldiers and temple officers with lanterns, torches, and weapons, He must have wondered what Judas was thinking or how he had erroneously perceived Him. Remember that the next time someone has had a wrong perception of you. If Jesus could be misunderstood, it can happen to you too, so don't let it ruffle your feathers too much.

In the next lesson, we'll learn the reason Judas gave Jesus a kiss of betrayal.

STUDY QUESTIONS

**Study to shew thyself approved unto God, a workman that
needeth not to be ashamed, rightly dividing the word of truth.
— 2 Timothy 2:15**

1. Scripture tells us that while He was in Gethsemane agonizing in prayer, Jesus asked the Father multiple times to do something. What was it? And what declaration did Jesus add to His request every time? (*See* Matthew 26:38-44; Mark 14:33-41; Luke 22:39-46.)

2. The scene in the Garden of Gethsemane is a vivid picture of Jesus wrestling with His human, fleshly nature — and gaining victory over it. What does this say to you about the fight with your own flesh? To learn how your spirit man can gain and maintain the upper hand over your flesh, take time to reflect on Paul's words in Romans 6; 8:1-17; 13:14; Galatians 5:16-25; Colossians 3:1-10,15,16.

3. Religious leaders tried to capture Jesus on numerous occasions, but each time, He miraculously escaped. Take a few moments to read about this in Luke 4:28-30; John 7:28-30; John 8:56-59; and John 10:31-39. What does this say to you about God's timing and His ability to protect you? As you answer, consider God's promises in Second Peter 2:9; First Corinthians 10:13; Second Timothy 4:18; and Psalm 91.

PRACTICAL APPLICATION

**But be ye doers of the word, and not hearers only,
deceiving your own selves.
— James 1:22**

1. One of the most extraordinary places near Jerusalem that few people know about is the Grotto of Gethsemane. Had you ever heard of this place prior to this lesson? What new details did you learn about this

cave, and how does it change the way you see Jesus and the events that took place in the Garden of Gethsemane?

2. What was most surprising and eye-opening to you when you learned the meaning and identity of the "band of men" and "officers" that accompanied Judas the night he betrayed Jesus? Why are the *lanterns*, *torches*, and *weapons* significant to understanding the magnitude of what took place the night of Jesus' arrest?

LESSON 3

TOPIC
The Judas Kiss

SCRIPTURES
1. **Mark 14:44** — And he that betrayed him had given them a token, saying, Whomsoever I shall kiss, that same is he; take him, and lead him away safely.
2. **Matthew 26:50** — And Jesus said unto him, Friend, wherefore art thou come? …
3. **Mark 14:45** — And as soon as he [Judas] was come, he goeth straightway to him, and saith, Master, master; and kissed him.
4. **John 13:13** — Ye call me Master and Lord: and ye say well; for so I am.
5. **John 18:4-6** — Jesus therefore, knowing all things that should come upon him, went forth, and said unto them, Whom seek ye? They answered him, Jesus of Nazareth. Jesus saith unto them, I am he…. As soon then as he had said unto them, I am he, they went backward, and fell to the ground.
6. **Exodus 3:14** — And God said unto Moses, I AM THAT I AM!
7. **John 18:6** — As soon then as he had said unto them, I am he [I AM], they went backward, and fell to the ground.

GREEK WORDS
1. "token" — (*sussemon*) a signal previously agreed upon

2. "friend" (*hetairos*) — a buddy, a companion, a comrade, a confidant, or an enjoyable friend; someone with whom one had spent much time and learned to enjoy

3. "kiss" (*phileso*) — strong affection, emotion, and love; affection primarily felt only between people who have a strong bond or a deeply felt obligation to each other, such as husbands and wives or family members; later, it came to be used as a form of greeting between especially dear and cherished friends; during the time that the gospels were written, it depicted friends who were bound by some kind of obligation or covenant and who cherished each other very deeply; also the word for a kiss that a man would give his wife, a kiss that parents and children might give to each other, or a kiss that a brother or sister might give to his or her siblings

4. "master" (*didaskalos*) — a fabulous, masterful teacher

5. "went backward" (*aperchomai*) — staggering and stumbling backward, as if some force had hit them and was pushing them back

6. "fell" (*pipto*) — to fall; often depicts a person who fell so hard, it appeared that he fell dead or fell like a corpse

7. "to the ground" (*chamai*) — hitting the ground hard

SYNOPSIS

Accompanied by a small army of 300 to 600 fully armed Roman soldiers and an untold number of fearsome temple police officers sent by the chief priests and Pharisees, Judas found Jesus in the Grotto of Gethsemane where He and His disciples frequently retreated. It was in that cave that Judas betrayed the Lord with a kiss, signaling to the soldiers the one they were to arrest and take away safely. But why a kiss? What was the significance of Judas' gesture, and what else can we learn from his actions?

The emphasis of this lesson:

Judas' kiss was a devised signal to let the troops know who they needed to arrest. His loyalty to Jesus was fatally flawed from the beginning. In Judas' heart and mind, Jesus was his 'Teacher' but never his 'Lord.'

Judas Met With Jewish Leaders, Plotting To Deliver Jesus Into Their Hands

Before Judas led a cohort of Roman soldiers and temple police to the grotto in the Garden of Gethsemane to arrest Jesus that night, he convened with the Jewish religious leaders to negotiate a deal for him to hand Jesus over to them.

During a clandestine meeting with these religious leaders, Judas disclosed to them where Jesus met with His disciples and where they could arrest Him in private, away from the eyes of the crowds that always followed Jesus. In that meeting, Judas agreed to receive a payment of 30 pieces of silver for betraying Jesus into their hands. This is recorded in Matthew 26:14-16 and 27:3-10.

It is likely that Judas also warned them about Jesus' phenomenal power, which would explain why a cohort of Roman soldiers — which was 300 to 600 armed warriors — came with the dreaded temple police to arrest Jesus on the night of His betrayal. Can you imagine a nearly 600-member militia showing up in a small cave to take Jesus into custody? That grotto must have been jam-packed with so many soldiers that they were spilling over into the stone passageway.

Indeed, Jesus' power was legendary. Stories of the miracles He had performed had gone out everywhere. Yet, because most of the soldiers and temple police had never actually seen Jesus themselves, Judas devised a signal to alert them of who Jesus was on that night. We find this described in Mark 14:44:

> **And he that betrayed him had given them a token, saying, Whomsoever I shall kiss, that same is he; take him, and lead him away safely.**

Notice the word "token" in this passage. In the original Greek, it describes *a signal previously agreed upon.* Judas' kiss was a pre-determined, devised signal to let the troops know who they needed to arrest.

Judas' Actions Demonstrate That Deceived People Are Confused People

Think of how confused Judas must have been. On one hand, he seemed to have warned the religious leaders about Jesus' supernatural power so effectively that the Romans soldiers and temple police arrived on the scene with weapons of murder, and they were prepared to put up a serious fight. On the other hand, Judas was sure that he could deliver Jesus into their hands with a mere *kiss*.

His actions demonstrate how *deceived people are always confused people*, and clearly, Judas was very confused.

Has anyone in your life ever done something to you that was completely shocking? For a long time, that person may have seen you and treated you as a good friend, and everything may have seemed to be going fine. But then, suddenly, maybe the script flipped, and in that person's mind you became an enemy. That type of behavior is indicative of one who is deceived and confused.

What Kind of Relationship Did Jesus and Judas Have?

During the three years of Jesus' ministry, Judas Iscariot had been the treasurer for the ministry, which meant he and Jesus had a close working relationship. They probably spent many hours together sitting side by side as they discussed ministry expenditures and ministry projects, such as how to help the poor and the needy.

The fact that Judas had spent so much time with Jesus means he really should have known who Jesus was. These two were so close that Jesus used a word to describe Judas that He didn't use anywhere else in the gospels. On that night He was betrayed, Jesus stepped forward to greet Judas, and Matthew records:

> **And Jesus said unto him, *Friend*, wherefore art thou come…?**
> **— Matthew 26:50**

The original Greek word for "friend" in this passage is the word for *a buddy, a companion, a comrade, a confidant,* or *an enjoyable friend*. It was someone with whom one had spent much time and learned to enjoy. Jesus' use of this word tells us He really liked Judas and He had worked so closely with him that He could call him a buddy, a companion, a comrade, a confidant, or an enjoyable friend.

Sadly, Judas' loyalty to Jesus was fatally flawed from the very beginning, which is what caused him to be deceived and make a deal with the devilish chief priests and Pharisees. Remember, Judas had previously told the Roman troops and temple police, "Whomsoever I shall kiss, that same is he; take him, and lead him away safely" (Mark 14:44).

What's in a 'Kiss'?

Pay attention to that word "kiss." It is a form of the word *phileo*, which means *to love like a friend*. In this verse, it is the Greek word *phileso*, which describes *strong affection, emotion, and love*. It is *affection primarily felt only between people who have a strong bond or a deeply felt obligation to each other, such as husbands and wives or family members*. Later, this word *phileso* came to be used as a form of greeting between especially dear and cherished friends.

During the time that the gospels were written, the word *phileso* depicted friends who were bound by some kind of obligation or covenant and who cherished each other very deeply. It is also the word for *a kiss that a man would give his wife*, or *a kiss that parents and children might give to each other*, or *a kiss that a brother or sister might give to his or her siblings*.

Hence, the word "kiss" was a symbol of deep love, affection, obligation, covenant, and relationship. This kind of kiss was such a powerful signal to everyone who saw it that strangers never greeted each other with such a kiss. It was a special kiss reserved only for the most treasured relationships.

Judas was aware that he could give Jesus such a kiss, which tells us what kind of relationship existed between them. They had been very closely connected as they worked on finances, talked about the distribution of funds, and strategized ways to help the poor and the needy. Indeed, they had a very enjoyable relationship.

Even though Jesus knew Judas had issues and was His betrayer, He nonetheless loved Judas to the point that Jesus called him "friend" when he entered the garden that night.

But the kiss Judas gave Jesus was a false kiss that revealed insincerity, bogus love, and a phony commitment. Judas played the game all the way to the end, working closely with Jesus and remaining a part of His inner circle, and then — at the pre-appointed time — he drove the dagger in as deeply as he could in the moment of betrayal in the Garden of Gethsemane.

Betraying Jesus with a kiss was about as low as a person could go. It was like saying, "You and I are friends forever. Now please turn around so I can sink my dagger into your back!"

In Judas' Heart and Mind
Jesus Was 'Teacher' But Never 'Lord'

Again, Judas' relationship with Jesus was flawed from the beginning, and this is confirmed in Mark 14:45, which says, "And as soon as he [Judas] was come, he goeth straightway to him, and saith, Master, master; and kissed him."

Notice that twice Judas called Jesus "master." In Greek, this word describes *a fabulous, masterful teacher.* Hence, this is the equivalent of Judas saying, "Teacher, teacher." It is important to notice that Judas didn't call Jesus "Lord."

Titles are very important because they define relationships.

The words "Daddy" and "mother" define the unique relationship between a child and a parent. The word "boss" defines the relationship between an employee and his employer — a relationship much different from the one that exists between the employee and his fellow employees.

Likewise, the words "Mr. President" define the relationship between a nation and its leader. The word "pastor" defines the relationship between a church congregation and their pastor. Again, titles provide definition, rank, and order to our relationships, and a world without titles would be a world with confusion.

In the gospels, we find that the apostles called Jesus "Lord."

That was the title they used. Earlier in His ministry, Jesus commended His disciples for this choice of title, saying, "Ye call me Master and Lord: and ye say well; for so I am" (John 13:13). Interestingly, there isn't a single occurrence in the gospels where the disciples casually called Jesus "Jesus." They were always respectful and honored Him.

The Greek word for "Lord" used throughout the New Testament is *Kurios,* and it expresses the idea of *one who has ultimate and supreme authority in every realm of one's life.* Thus, when the disciples called Jesus "Lord," it meant they were submitted to His authority and had yielded every area of their existence to His management, direction, and control. The same is true for you when you call Jesus "Lord."

If Judas had called Jesus "Lord" that night, it would have meant he had surrendered his life to Jesus' control and was submitted to His Lordship and authority, but that wasn't the case. On the night that Judas showed up in the Garden of Gethsemane, he didn't call Jesus "Lord." Instead, he called Him "Master," which essentially means "Fabulous Teacher." This revealed that though Judas respected Jesus as a Teacher, a Rabbi, and a gifted communicator, Jesus had never really become Lord in Judas' life. The devil knew that, and that is how he gained access into Judas (*see* Luke 22:3; John 13:27).

It is unthinkable that Judas Iscariot, who once had a cherished relationship with Jesus, could become so deceived that he would betray Him with a kiss! Just imagine! With a phony, bogus kiss, Judas delivered Jesus into the hands of Roman forces and to Caiaphas, the high priest, and the scribes and Pharisees.

As happens in all relationships where submission to authority is required, a moment finally came that revealed the true level of Judas' relationship with Jesus, and it revealed that there was a fatal flaw.

Jesus Was — and Is — God in the Flesh!

Immediately after receiving Judas' kiss of betrayal, Jesus stepped forward to ask the crowd of militia, "…Whom seek ye? They answered him, Jesus of Nazareth. Jesus saith unto them, I am he. And Judas also, which betrayed him, stood with them. As soon then as he had said unto them, I am he, they went backward, and fell to the ground" (John 18:4-6).

Pay attention to the words "I am he," which appear twice in this passage. This is a translation of the Greek words *Ego eimi*, and it literally means *I AM*. These words "I am," the Greek phrase *Egō eimi*, are the exact same words found in Exodus 3:14, when God said to Moses, "…I AM THAT I AM."

This was not the only time Jesus used the words *Egō eimi*. In John 8:58, when He responded to the Pharisees, He declared, "…Verily, verily, I say unto you, Before Abraham was, *I am*." These words were a statement acknowledging who He was. Jesus was declaring that He was — *and still is* — God in the flesh. By using this well-known phrase, Jesus was declaring to these hundreds of Roman soldiers and temple police officers, "I am the Great I AM of the Old Testament. I am the I AM, which was before Abraham. I AM God in the flesh!"

The Soldiers and Temple Police Were Knocked Flat by Jesus' Power

According to John 18:6, when Jesus made it clear He was the Great "I AM" of the Bible, the group of men who had come to capture Jesus "…went backward, and fell to the ground." The phrase "went backward" means *to stagger and stumble backward*. It was as if some force had hit Jesus' captors and was pushing them backward. The invisible force of the power of God was too strong for the soldiers to remain standing, so they were pushed backward and fell to the ground.

The word "fell" is a form of the Greek word *pipto*, which means *to fall*, and it often depicts a person who fell so hard, it appeared that he *fell dead* or *fell like a corpse*. The crowd of militia fell like corpses, and they fell "to the ground." This phrase is a translation of the Greek word *chamai*, which depicts *falling abruptly and hitting the ground hard*.

Can you imagine! These 300 to 600 fully armed soldiers and officers were knocked flat by some kind of invisible force. When Jesus said, "I AM!" a blast of God's power was unleashed so strongly that it literally thrust the troops and temple police backward, causing them to stagger, wobble, and stumble as they hit the ground hard.

The tales they had heard about Jesus' supernatural power were correct! All Jesus had to do was identify who He was. He said, "I AM — *Ego eimi*!" He really was strong enough to overcome an army. But after Jesus proved He couldn't be taken by force, He then willfully surrendered to them.

Friend, it is vital to understand that no one *took* Jesus. It was His voluntary choice to go with the troops because He knew it was a part of the Father's plan for the redemption of mankind. There is no force strong enough to resist His power. No sickness, no substance, no financial turmoil, no habit, no relational problems, no political force — absolutely *nothing* has enough power to resist the supernatural power of Jesus Christ!

When Jesus opens His mouth and speaks, every power that attempts to defy Him or His Word is pushed backward and shaken until it staggers, stumbles, and falls to the ground! So what is your need today? Present it to Jesus and let Him speak His Word over your life. You will see the mighty power of God unleashed against the evil forces that have been trying to defy you!

STUDY QUESTIONS

Study to shew thyself approved unto God, a workman that
needeth not to be ashamed, rightly dividing the word of truth.
— 2 Timothy 2:15

1. Take a few moments to reread the section "What's in a 'Kiss'?" How does the meaning of the word *phileo* (kiss) expand your perspective of Judas' actions? If you were on the receiving end of such a *kiss*, how would it make you feel and how might you react? Would you call Judas "friend" as Jesus did?

2. The Bible says that Jesus is THE WORD of God made flesh (*see* John 1:1,14). When He opened His mouth, power was released! Likewise, when you open your mouth and speak God's Word, power is released. Take a moment to meditate on the words of Proverbs 18:21 and Jeremiah 23:28 and 29. What is the Holy Spirit telling you through this passage?

PRACTICAL APPLICATION

But be ye doers of the word, and not hearers only,
deceiving your own selves.
— James 1:22

1. Has anyone in your life ever done something to you that was completely shocking? For a long time, that person may have seen you and treated you as a good friend, and everything may have seemed to be going fine. But then, suddenly, maybe the script flipped, and in that person's mind you became an enemy. If this has ever happened to you, how does Jesus' interaction with Judas help you better understand and respond to your situation?

2. The Greek word for "Lord" used throughout the New Testament is *Kurios*, and it expresses the idea of *one who has ultimate and supreme authority in every realm of one's life*. Be honest with yourself, is Jesus Christ truly LORD of your life? Are you really submitted to His authority, and have you yielded every area of your existence to His management, direction, and control? If not, what areas do you need to let go of and surrender to Him?

3. There's no force strong enough to resist Jesus' power! No sickness, no substance, no financial turmoil, no habit, no relational problems, no

political force — absolutely nothing has enough power to resist the divine power of Jesus Christ! What do you need today? Present it to Jesus! Cast your cares on Him (*see* 1 Peter 5:7). Speak His Word over your life daily, and you'll see the mighty power of God unleashed against the evil forces that have been trying to defy you!

TOPIC

Peter's Mess and the Naked Boy in the Garden of Gethsemane

SCRIPTURES

1. **Luke 22:49** — ...Lord, shall we smite with the sword?
2. **John 18:10** — Then Simon Peter having a sword drew it, and smote the high priest's servant, and cut off his right ear. The servant's name was Malchus.
3. **Luke 22:51** — And Jesus answered and said, Suffer ye thus far. And he touched his ear, and healed him.
4. **Matthew 26:53** — Thinkest thou that I cannot now pray to my Father, and he shall presently give me more than twelve legions of angels?
5. **Mark 14:51,52** — And there followed him a certain young man, having a linen cloth cast about his naked body; and the young men laid hold on him: and he left the linen cloth, and fled from them naked.
6. **John 19:11** — Jesus answered, Thou couldest have no power at all against me, except it were given thee from above....

GREEK WORDS

1. "smote" (*epaio*) — to strike, as a person who viciously strikes someone with a dangerous tool, weapon, or instrument; it can also be translated to sting, like a scorpion that strongly injects its stinger into a victim; to beat with the fist; this word pictures the force of Peter's swinging action and tells us Peter put all his strength into the swinging of his sword, doing it with the full intention of causing bodily impairment

2. "cut off" (*apokopto*) — a downward swing that cuts something off
3. "ear" (*otarion*) — the entire outer ear
4. "touched" (*aptomai*) — to firmly grasp or to hold tightly
5. "healed" (*iaomai*)— to cure, to restore, or to heal
6. "followed" (*sunakoloutheo*) — to continuously follow
7. "linen cloth" (*sindon*) — used to depict the linen cloth in which the body of Jesus was wrapped for burial; this was a burial shroud used for covering a dead body in the grave

SYNOPSIS

Have you ever acted rashly and really made a mess of things in your life? You are not alone. We have all been guilty of acting thoughtlessly and foolishly. Hotheaded moments rarely produce good fruit. When we act recklessly, we usually end up loathing the stupidity of our words and actions.

That is what happened to Peter in the Garden of Gethsemane the night of Jesus' arrest. No story better demonstrates the mess that impatience produces than when Peter seized a sword, swung it with all his might, and lopped off the ear of the high priest's servant.

But Jesus loved Peter immensely and chose to step in and clean up his mess. If you have made a mess of things in the past and you're reaping the consequences of it right now, hope is not lost. Jesus loves you beyond words and stands ready to put the pieces of your life back together. As you lean into this lesson, invite His presence into your situation and watch Him work wonders for you!

The emphasis of this lesson:

Peter's reckless behavior of attacking the high priest's servant was criminal and deserving of imprisonment. But Jesus stepped in and restored Malchus' ear and Peter's future through one healing touch. And although Jesus could have called on the power of 12 legions of angels to come to His defense, He didn't — He gave Himself up willingly.

A Quick Review of Lesson 3

In our last lesson, we saw that when Judas came to the Grotto of Gethsemane the night he betrayed Jesus, he brought a small army with him.

Altogether, there were likely more than 600 fully armed Roman soldiers and temple police officers who came to arrest Jesus, and Judas' kiss was the devised signal to confirm who they were to take into custody.

Once the soldiers made it clear that they were looking for "Jesus of Nazareth," Jesus answered and said, "I am he," and "As soon then as he had said unto them, I am he, they went backward, and fell to the ground" (John 18:5,6). The words "I am he" in Greek are the words *Ego eimi*, which literally means *I AM*. By using this familiar expression, Jesus identified Himself as the Great I AM of the Old Testament, and when He spoke these words, power was released that was so intense it knocked all the armed forces flat to the ground!

Without question, Jesus' power was legendary — even during His lifetime. And when that power was detonated through His words, all the stories these men had heard about Jesus' might were confirmed. The Bible says that in the very near future, when Jesus returns to the earth at His Second Coming, He will incinerate the antichrist with the power of His word (*see* 2 Thessalonians 2:8).

Friend, if you have a need or you're facing an attack, grab hold of the Word of God and begin declaring it out loud over your life and against the enemy! Remember, the same Spirit that raised Christ from the dead lives in you (*see* Romans 8:11). So when you openly declare God's Word, the Word of His power can obliterate anything and everything that is coming against you.

Acting in Haste, Peter Cut off the Ear of the High Priest's Servant

As hundreds of soldiers and police officers were lying flat on the ground, dazed and disabled by the power released through Jesus' words, Peter impetuously tried to take matters into his own hands. His spontaneous, hasty behavior earned him a place in history that no one has ever forgotten.

It seems that at some point, either in the Grotto of Gethsemane or out in the garden itself, Peter did the unthinkable. When he saw the mob laying on the ground, incapacitated by the power of God, he got a crazy idea and swung into action without thinking. To see the full picture of what took place that night, we need to piece the story together from Luke's and John's gospels.

In Luke 22:49, we find that Peter pulled out a sword and asked, "…Lord, shall we smite with the sword?" When he saw the Roman soldiers and religious police officers laying paralyzed on the ground, he viewed it as an opportunity to take revenge on his enemies, which he had probably wanted to do for a long time.

Before Jesus could answer, Peter grabbed a sword, swung down, and cut the ear off the high priest's servant. John 18:10 confirms this, telling us:

> **Then Simon Peter having a sword drew it, and smote the high priest's servant, and cut off his right ear. The servant's name was Malchus.**

The word "smote" in this verse is very important. In Greek, it means *to strike, as a person who viciously strikes someone with a dangerous tool, weapon, or instrument.* It can be translated *to sting*, like a scorpion that strongly injects its stinger into a victim. Moreover, the word "smote" can mean *to beat with the fist.* In John 18:10, it pictures the force of Peter's swinging action and tells us Peter put all his strength into the swinging of that sword and did it with the full intention to cause bodily impairment.

Do you really think Peter was aiming for the servant's ear? Why would anyone attack another person's *ear* — especially if you were trying to take revenge? The truth is Peter was most likely aiming for the servant's head and missed, cutting off his right ear by mistake.

The words "cut off" in the original Greek describe *a downward swing that cuts something off*, and the word "ear" indicates *the entire outer ear*. So now in front of Jesus was a wounded man who had blood pouring from the side of his head. You can probably imagine him lifting his hand in utter shock, trying to apply pressure to the side of his head to stop the bleeding as he looked at his severed ear laying on the ground to his side.

An Overview of Caiaphas the High Priest and His Servant Malchus

The Bible identifies the man Peter attacked as Malchus (*see* John 18:10). Although we don't know much about Malchus, here's what we do know:

- The name "Malchus" has two meanings: *ruler* and *counselor*.
- He was the personal assistant, or counselor, of Caiaphas, the high priest.

- Caiaphas hated Jesus, so more than likely, Malchus hated Jesus and His disciples.

Caiaphas was a member of the Sadducees, a religious sect that did not believe in the supernatural and who viewed the miraculous events of the Old Testament as myths and legends. This is one reason Caiaphas was so antagonistic to the ministry of Jesus, which, of course, was overflowing with miraculous events every day. Add to this the fact that he and the Jewish leaders were not able to control or manage Jesus' activities, and you can see why Caiaphas had been trying to capture Jesus and get rid of Him for quite some time.

As spokesman for the high priest, it is likely Malchus had been a public voice for Caiaphas, and as his mouthpiece, it was Malchus who previously issued atrocious statements about Jesus and his disciples. As a high-ranking officer of the religious court, he was regally dressed and carried himself with pride and dignity. To Peter's eye, he probably represented everything that belonged to the religious men who had instigated numerous problems for Jesus and His disciples.

When Peter saw Malchus make his way into Gethsemane, it likely brought back bad memories of the many times he had seen Malchus standing at the side of the high priest or the times he had issued public damning statements about Jesus. It is likely that Peter highly resented Malchus and had a long-held grudge against him, the high priest, and his entourage, all of whom had been critical of Jesus' ministry.

Few scholars believe that Peter singled Malchus out by chance. Rather, they believe Peter deliberately attacked him — swinging for his head but only managing to take off his ear.

Jesus Restored Two Lives
With One Healing Touch

What Peter did was a very serious matter. Not only was it scandalous, but it was also against the law. Malchus was a very well-known public figure, and Peter's actions against him were both criminal and punishable. He could be sent to prison for assaulting a public official.

It is also important to note that one who was disfigured was not allowed certain functions in holy sites. Thus, such a disfigurement would have prohibited Malchus from serving in the temple premises. So rather than leave him disfigured, Jesus stepped forward and healed him and protected his ability to serve in his profession alongside the high priest. The healing of Malchus' ear was the last miracle Jesus performed before his death, burial, and resurrection.

Think about it. Just before Jesus went to the Cross, He healed and helped one who had been His publicly-declared and avowed foe! When Malchus got his ear cut off, Jesus didn't say, "Finally, one of you guys got what you deserve!" Instead, Jesus reached out to this man in need, touched him, and healed him. What a contrast Jesus' actions were to Peter's behavior.

At the same time Jesus was healing one of His self-avowed enemies, He was also cleaning up Peter's mess. Again, Peter's actions were criminal and could have caused him to be prosecuted and imprisoned. Malchus was a high-profile public servant who had been publicly assaulted by Peter. Jesus knew this, and in His infinite wisdom and compassion, stepped in and cleaned up Peter's mess, knowing that Peter would help lead the Church Christ Himself was about to establish.

Keep in mind, just moments before…

- Jesus was agonizing in prayer on that outcropping of rock in the Garden of Gethsemane, sweating great drops of blood from an intense spiritual battle He was fighting in prayer.

- After intensely interceding and receiving supernatural strength from an angel, Jesus then received the kiss of betrayal from Judas, His very close friend.

- Now, a new problem was thrust upon Jesus because of Peter's rash behavior. Blood was pouring from the side of Malchus' head as Peter's hand grasped the blade that did the deed.

How did the Lord, the King of Glory, handle such an unprecedented series of events?

Jesus 'Touched' and 'Healed' Malchus

To answer this vital question, we turn our attention to the gospel of Luke, which says:

And Jesus answered and said, Suffer ye thus far. And he touched his ear, and healed him.

— Luke 22:51

First, notice the phrase, "Suffer ye thus far." Looking at the original language, we learn that this is the equivalent of Jesus saying, "Give me a minute…. Let Me just do one more thing before you take Me!" Then the Bible says Jesus "…touched his ear, and healed him" (Luke 22:51).

The Greek word for "touched" means *to firmly grasp or to hold tightly.* This tells us that Jesus firmly grabbed Malchus' head and held it tightly. With great tenacity, Jesus prayed for Malchus in the same way He prayed for others. When He laid His hands on people, they knew that hands had been laid on them!

As a result of Jesus' hands-on prayer, Malchus was *healed.* This word "healed" literally means *to cure, to restore,* or *to heal.* The Bible doesn't tell us if Jesus reached over, picked up the severed ear off the ground, and miraculously set it back in its place or if He touched Malchus' head and grew a brand-new ear on the stump that remained. Either way, by the time Jesus was finished, there was a brand-new ear on the right side of Malchus' head.

Jesus Had Access to Unparalleled Angelic Power But Refrained From Activating It

Indeed, the power that was on display in the Garden of Gethsemane that night was astounding! Hundreds of soldiers and temple police officers were knocked flat to the ground by the power of Jesus' words. A man's ear that was cut off in a vengeful fury was miraculously restored through Jesus' healing touch. And the incriminating evidence that could have put Peter in prison was miraculously erased by Jesus' restorative power.

But that wasn't all that happened in the Garden of Gethsemane that night. Right about the time Jesus had finished healing Malchus' ear and just before the soldiers brought Him into custody, Jesus made a very eye-opening statement that deserves our attention. It is recorded in Matthew 26:53. Here, Jesus said:

Thinkest thou that I cannot now pray to my Father, and he shall presently give me more than twelve legions of angels?

Slow down and reread what Jesus is saying here so you can really grab hold of its significance. Remember, it's Jesus who is speaking, so what He says is absolute truth, no exaggeration or hype. He told the hundreds of soldiers and temple police that with one prayer from His lips to the Father in Heaven, He would be given more than 12 legions of angels to help Him.

Since there are 6,000 in one legion, 12 legions of angels would equal 72,000 angels. Jesus said that the Father would send Him *more than* 12 legions of angels, which means more than 72,000 mighty, dazzling, glorious, powerful angels were on standby and ready to be instantly dispatched to the Garden of Gethsemane to obliterate the forces that came to arrest Jesus.

How powerful are these angels? Well, the Bible says in Isaiah 37:36 that one angel by himself killed 185,000 men in one night. If we multiply 72,000 angels by 185,000, we see that 12 legions of angels would have the combined force to kill 13,320,000,000 people, which is nearly twice the current population of the earth.

So Jesus didn't really need Peter's sword that night. He had the supernatural backup of more than 72,000 angels! But He didn't call for those angels to come to His aid because He knew it was the will of the Father for Him to die on the Cross as the Lamb of God.

Who Was the Naked Boy in the Garden of Gethsemane?

There is one more remarkable event that took place in the Garden of Gethsemane the night Jesus was arrested, and it is only briefly mentioned in two verses of Mark's gospel. Scripture says that as Jesus was being taken into custody...

> **...There followed him a certain young man, having a linen cloth cast about his naked body; and the young men laid hold on him: and he left the linen cloth, and fled from them naked**
> **— Mark 14:51,52**

Immediately after reading this passage, several questions come to mind: *Who was this young man? Why was he naked? And why was he draped in a linen cloth?* The key to understanding the identity of this young man is in understanding the meaning of the words "linen cloth." It is a translation of the Greek word *sindon*, which describes *a burial shroud used for covering a dead body in the grave.* This is the very word used in the gospels to depict the linen cloth in which the body of Jesus was wrapped for burial.

As we noted in a previous lesson, the Garden of Gethsemane, which is located on the lower slopes of the Mount of Olives, was home to a cemetery where wealthy people would bury their loved ones. To this day, at the base of the mount is a heavily populated cemetery, with many of its graves going back to the time of Jesus.

Apparently, this young man with only a linen cloth wrapped around his body was someone who had recently died. As was the Jewish custom, the boy's body was cleansed and prepared for burial, and he was then placed in the grave naked, wrapped in the traditional burial shroud.

When Jesus identified Himself as "I AM," and power was released that knocked all the soldiers and police officers flat to the ground, evidently, it also caused a rumbling in the local cemetery! The blast of power that was detonated through Jesus' words also raised this young man from the dead! Suddenly and unexpectedly, life returned to his body, and he came crawling out of his tomb draped in a linen burial cloth!

Returning to Mark 14:51, we read that the young man "…there followed him [Jesus]…." The word "followed" describes an ongoing action. Hence, the young man *kept following and following and following* Jesus, possibly wondering why he had come back to life and who was Jesus.

The passage goes on to say, "…And the young men laid hold on him: and he left the linen cloth, and fled from them naked" (Mark 14:51,52). At some point, as the young man was pursuing Jesus and the mob of militia that were taking Him away, some of the soldiers discovered he was following Jesus, and they tried to arrest him. Clearly, the last thing the temple police and the Roman soldiers wanted was another story of Jesus' legendary power reaching the public.

To prevent news of this young man's peripheral resurrection from getting out, the soldiers attempted to nab him. But when they reached out to grab him, he swiftly fled the scene and left the linen cloth in their hands.

No One Took Jesus' Life...
He Willingly Surrendered It

Friend, there was enormous supernatural power at work all over the Garden of Gethsemane the night of Jesus' betrayal. In fact, there was so much power present that no one could have withstood Jesus had He chosen to resist. Basically, that is what Jesus told Pilate when He stood trial before him. According to John 19:11:

> **Jesus answered, Thou couldest have no power at all against me, except it were given thee from above....**

Jesus was not taken by the will of man. No one had sufficient power to forcibly take Him. The only reason He was taken into custody and sentenced to death was because He chose to willingly lay down His life for you and all of mankind. In John 10:17 and 18 (*TLB*), Jesus said:

> **The Father loves me because I lay down my life that I may have it back again. No one can kill me without my consent — I lay down my life voluntarily. For I have the right and power to lay it down when I want to and also the right and power to take it again. For the Father has given me this right.**

Jesus knew it was the Father's will that He die on the Cross as the Lamb of God and pay the penalty for our sins. But He also knew that on the third day, He would be raised back to life to the glory of God!

STUDY QUESTIONS

> **Study to shew thyself approved unto God, a workman that needeth not to be ashamed, rightly dividing the word of truth.**
> **— 2 Timothy 2:15**

1. What new information did you learn about Caiaphas the high priest and his servant Malchus? How do you see Peter's sword-swinging scene in the Garden of Gethsemane with new eyes?

2. Take a few moments to contemplate all the dynamics of what Jesus was dealing with on the night He was betrayed in the Garden of Gethsemane:
   - As He agonized and wrestled in prayer, His closest friends fell asleep.

- After sweating blood, He was given a bogus kiss and was betrayed by a very close friend.
- While walking out God's will, another close friend went berserk and created a bloody mess.
- Even after tangibly displaying great supernatural power before their eyes, Jesus' enemies still arrested Him and led Him away to trial.

How is your view of Jesus impacted when you stop to think about all He endured that night?

PRACTICAL APPLICATION

**But be ye doers of the word, and not hearers only,
deceiving your own selves.
—James 1:22**

1. As you read through Jesus' words in Matthew 26:53 where He described the unparalleled angelic power He had instant access to, how does His unbelievable level of restraint help you better understand His indescribable love for you? (*Consider* Romans 5:6-8; 1 John 3:16; Ephesians 5:2.)

2. Is there a "Malchus" in your life? Is there a person who, at the sight of his or her face or the hearing of that person's name, brings back bad memories? If so, who is it and what did he or she do that is so hurtful and even treacherous in your mind? Pour out your thoughts and feelings to God (Psalm 62:8).

3. If you are still dealing with the raw emotions of pain and anger over what someone did, it is likely that you are holding onto offense and unforgiveness. To move forward and experience all the good things God has in store for you, make the choice to begin the process of forgiveness.

Biblical Steps To Walking in Forgiveness
- Admit that you are offended and with whom you are offended.
- (Proverbs 28:13; Ezekiel 18:31; 1 John 1:7-10)
- Release the person and his or her offense to God; make the daily choice to forgive.
- (Matthew 6:14,15; Mark 11:25; Ephesians 4:32; Colossians 3:13)

- Ask for and receive God's forgiveness for holding onto offense and unforgiveness.
- (Psalm 32:1-6; Proverbs 28:13; Acts 3:19; 1 John 1:9)
- Bless the person who hurt you; as an act of your will, pray for God to bless that person.
- (Matthew 5:44,45; Romans 12:14; 1 Peter 3:8-12)

Remember, forgiving someone is a *process*, so repeat these steps as often as necessary, especially when thoughts of what they did return and/or you feel negative emotions trying to rise up and take root again. God will honor and bless your efforts to walk in forgiveness!

LESSON 5

TOPIC

Spitting in Jesus' Face and Playing Games With Jesus

SCRIPTURES

1. **Matthew 26:57** — And they that had laid hold on Jesus led him away to Caiaphas the high priest, where the scribes and the elders were assembled.

2. **Isaiah 53:7** — He is brought as a lamb to the slaughter, and as a sheep before her shearers is dumb, so he openeth not his mouth.

3. **2 Corinthians 5:21** — For he hath made him to be sin for us, who knew no sin; that we might be made the righteousness of God in him.

4. **1 Peter 2:22** — Who did no sin, neither was guile found in his mouth.

5. **Acts 10:38** — How God anointed Jesus of Nazareth with the Holy Ghost and with power: who went about doing good, and healing all that were oppressed of the devil; for God was with him [Jesus].

6. **1 Peter 2:23** — Who, when he was reviled, reviled not again; when he suffered, he threatened not; but committed himself to him that judgeth righteously.

7. **Matthew 26:64** — Jesus saith unto him, Thou hast said: nevertheless I say unto you, Hereafter shall ye see the Son of man sitting on the right hand of power, and coming in the clouds of heaven.

8. **Matthew 26:66** — ...They answered and said, He is guilty of death.

9. **Matthew 26:67,68** — Then did they spit in his face, and buffeted him; and others smote him with the palms of their hands, saying, Prophesy unto us, thou Christ, Who is he that smote thee?

10. **Luke 22:63** — And the men that held Jesus mocked him, and smote him. And when they had blindfolded him, they struck him on the face, and asked him, saying, Prophesy, who is it that smote thee? And many other things blasphemously spake they against him.

11. **Matthew 23:27** — Woe unto you, scribes and Pharisees, hypocrites! for ye are like unto whited sepulchres, which indeed appear beautiful outward, but are within full of dead men's bones, and of all uncleanness.

GREEK WORDS

1. "laid hold" (*kratos*) — to seize, to take hold of, to firmly grip, or to apprehend; in this context, it carries the idea of making a forceful arrest

2. "led him away" (*apago*) — pictures a shepherd who ties a rope around the neck of his sheep and then leads it down the path to where it needs to go

3. "committed" (*paradidomai*) — to commend; to commit; to deliver; to transmit; to yield; to deliver; or to hand something over to someone else

4. "buffeted"(*kolaphidzo*) — to strike with the fist; pictures a person who is violently beaten

5. "mocked" (*empaidzo*) — to play a game with children or to amuse a crowd by impersonating someone in a silly and exaggerated way; for instance, this word could be used to depict a game of charades when someone intends to comically portray a person or even make fun of someone

6. "smote" (*dero*) — the grueling and barbaric practice of beating a slave; a word so dreadful that it is often translated to flay, such as to flay the flesh from an animal or human being

7. "blindfolded"(*perikalupto*) — to wrap a veil or garment about someone, thus hiding his eyes so he can't see

8. "struck" (*paio*) — a strike that stings; they slapped Him on the face
9. "blasphemously" (*blasphemeo*) — to accuse; to speak against; to slander; to speak derogatory words for the purpose of injuring or harming one's reputation; signifies profane, foul, unclean language

SYNOPSIS

Despised, rejected, and acquainted with grief — that is Jesus' biography that was penned in Isaiah 53:3. If ever anyone was qualified to understand the difficulties you are going through — and provide strength to make it through — *it is Jesus*.

Because He has "been there and done that," Jesus "…is able [immediately] to run to the cry of (assist, relieve) those who are being tempted and tested and tried [and who therefore are being exposed to suffering]" (Hebrews 2:18 *AMPC*). As you make your way through this fifth lesson, may your heart and mind be deeply moved with a fresh revelation of what Jesus went through for you.

The emphasis of this lesson:

Jesus allowed the soldiers to take Him into custody where Caiaphas and about 100 religious leaders physically abused, blasphemed, and mocked Jesus and then permitted the temple police to do the same. Through it all, Jesus entrusted Himself to God's care.

Here Is What We Know So Far…

In our previous lessons, we have seen the tremendous power of Jesus Christ working through His life — even at the time of His arrest. After Judas Iscariot made a deal to hand Jesus over to the religious leaders for 30 pieces of silver, he led 300 to 600 Roman soldiers plus a host of temple police officers into the Grotto of Gethsemane to arrest Jesus.

Mighty power was released through Jesus' words.

Judas stepped forward toward Jesus and gave Him a fake kiss, which was really a kiss of betrayal. The Bible then says, "Jesus therefore, knowing all things that should come upon him, went forth, and said unto them, Whom seek ye? They answered him, Jesus of Nazareth. Jesus saith unto them, I am he. And…as soon then as he had said unto them, I am he, they went backward, and fell to the ground" (John 18:4-6).

Jesus' declaration, "I am He," is a translation of the Greek phrase *Ego eimi*, which means *I AM*, and it is the same words used in Exodus 3:14 when God told Moses that His name is "I AM THAT I AM." When Jesus identified Himself to those armed forces as "I AM," He was declaring who He really was and still is — the Great I AM of the Old Testament, God in the flesh!

The moment Jesus spoke those words, they "went backward, and fell to the ground" (John 18:6). The word "fell" is a form of the Greek word *pipto*, which means *to fall so hard that it appears one has fallen dead or has fallen like a corpse*. The phrase "to the ground" is the Greek word *chamai*, and it depicts *falling abruptly and hitting the ground hard.*

There was such a release of divine power in that moment that the hundreds upon hundreds of soldiers and temple police were pushed backward and to the ground. The meaning of the Greek text here depicts this mob of militia stumbling, staggering, and wobbling until they can no longer resist the invisible force coming against them. Thus, they fell to the ground as dead men.

Peter recklessly took matters into His own hands.

At that point, Peter did something very impetuous. It seems that when he saw all these armed men laying on the ground, among them was a man named Malchus, the servant and public spokesman of the high priest who had a reputation for saying many atrocious things about Jesus and the rest of the disciples.

When Peter saw that Malchus had been knocked to the ground and had been dazed and confused by the power of God, he couldn't resist the temptation. So he reached for a sword and tried to cut off Malchus' head, but because he was a fisherman and not a swordsman, he only managed to cut off Malchus' ear.

Jesus stepped in and cleaned up Peter's mess.

As Jesus stood and watched this whole drama play out, He "...answered and said, Suffer ye thus far..." (Luke 22:51), which was the same as Him saying, "Give me a minute.... Let Me just do one more thing before you take Me!" Then the Bible says that Jesus touched Malchus' ear and healed him (*see* Luke 22:51).

The Greek word for "touched" means *to firmly grasp or to hold tightly*, which tells us Jesus firmly grabbed Malchus' head, held it tightly, and released healing to his ear. Malchus either regrew an ear or Jesus picked up the ear that was lopped off and put it back on. Either way, a miracle took place.

The power of Jesus' words also resurrected a dead boy.

Then as the soldiers were taking Jesus away, another miracle took place. Suddenly, a naked boy with only a linen cloth wrapped around himself showed up out of nowhere. This account is only recorded in Mark 14:51 and 52.

The key to understanding who this young man was and why he was in the garden is found in the meaning of the words "linen cloth." In Greek, these words describe *a burial shroud* that was used to wrap around a loved one who had passed away.

Apparently, this young man with only a linen cloth wrapped around his body was someone who had recently died and had been buried in the cemetery in Gethsemane. The Jews customarily buried their dead naked and covered them with a linen cloth. That's also how Jesus was buried.

When Jesus spoke the words "I AM," and power was released that knocked all the soldiers and police officers flat to the ground, evidently that same power also caused a rumbling in the local cemetery. It was a blast so strong that it brought this young man, who was once dead, back to life! And he came crawling out of his tomb draped in only the linen cloth in which he had been buried.

When the troops bringing Jesus to trial saw the boy in the burial shroud trailing behind them, they tried to grab him because they didn't want the news of another resurrection being noised abroad. But the young man was too fast, and he escaped their grasp, leaving them holding his linen cloth in their hands.

Jesus allowed the soldiers to take Him into custody.

After Jesus demonstrated His power in Gethsemane, He willingly permitted the soldiers to take Him into custody and lead Him to Caiaphas and other religious leaders who abused Him and poured their hate out toward him.

In a certain sense, letting the soldiers take Him into custody was simply an act, for He'd already vividly proven that they didn't have adequate power to take Him. Just one word and He had put all the soldiers on their backs. And if He wanted to stop the whole charade, He could have prayed to the Father and instantly activated 12 legions of angels to come to His aid. But He didn't. The Bible says:

And they that had laid hold on Jesus led him away to Caiaphas the high priest, where the scribes and the elders were assembled.
— Matthew 26:57

The words "laid hold" mean *to seize, to take hold of, to firmly grip*, or *to apprehend*. In this context, it carries the idea of making a forceful arrest. In the futile minds of these men, they believed they were in control of Jesus, but it was really Jesus surrendering to their plans to bring about the redemption of mankind.

When the Bible says they "led him away," it is a form of the Greek word *ago*, which pictures *a shepherd who ties a rope around the neck of his sheep and then leads it down the path to where it needs to go*. Jesus surrendered to the soldiers and allowed them to slip a rope about His neck and lead Him down the path as He followed behind, just like a sheep being led by a shepherd.

This is a fulfillment of something Isaiah prophesied about Jesus many centuries earlier. In Isaiah 53:7, it says, "…He is brought as a lamb to the slaughter, and as a sheep before her shearers is dumb, so he openeth not his mouth." This verse was fulfilled as Jesus was led like a lamb to the slaughter, and in a few moments, we will see how He refused to open His mouth and defend Himself as religious leaders blasphemed and abused Him.

Caiaphas Was the First Authority to Whom Jesus Was Brought

The first leader Jesus was led to on that dreadful night was a man named Caiaphas. He was a Sadducee, which was a group of liberal religious leaders who did not believe in the supernatural. They worked hard to debunk most of the supernatural occurrences in the Old Testament as merely myths and fantasies.

This helps us understand why Caiaphas and his religious sect had such hatred for Jesus. Indeed, the constant reports of Jesus' supernatural powers and miracles caused Caiaphas to view the Lord as a threat. These religious leaders were control freaks, and it was an outrage to them that Jesus' ministry was beyond their control. And whatever they couldn't control they tried to destroy.

As high priest, Caiaphas was responsible for arranging an illegal trial before the Jewish authorities to charge Jesus with a crime that would eventually cause Him to be crucified. Specifically, Caiaphas charged Jesus with the sin of blasphemy because He had called Himself the Son of God. When it became apparent that this accusation was not provable, Caiaphas delivered Jesus to the Roman authorities, who then found Him guilty of treason for claiming to be the king of the Jews.

To be clear — **JESUS NEVER SINNED!**

- Second Corinthians 5:21 says, "For he hath made him to be sin for us, who *knew no sin*; that we might be made the righteousness of God in him."
- First Peter 2:22 says, "[Christ] *Who did no sin*, neither was guile found in his mouth."

Make no mistake. Jesus' entire life was devoted to serving the needs of others. Acts 10:38 confirms this saying, "How God anointed Jesus of Nazareth with the Holy Ghost and with power: who went about doing good, and healing all that were oppressed of the devil; for God was with him."

Jesus Trusted Himself Into the Care of the Father

Even though Jesus did not sin, He was temporarily placed into the hands of evil spiritual vipers in Jerusalem to fulfill the will of God and carry out the plan for man's salvation. And at the same time, Jesus entrusted Himself into the hands of the Father. Speaking of Jesus' response to all the attacks brought against Him, Peter wrote:

> **Who, when he was reviled, reviled not again; when he suffered, he threatened not; but committed himself to him that judgeth righteously.**
>
> **— 1 Peter 2:23**

The word "committed" in this verse is a form of the Greek word *paradidomai*, which means *to commend; to commit; to deliver; to transmit; to yield;* or *to hand something over to someone else.* In those moments, when Jesus was being brutally mistreated and found Himself in an unjust situation, He completely committed Himself to the One who judges righteously. In that difficult hour, He drew near to the Father — fully entrusting Himself and His future into His Father's hands — and leaving the results in His control. That is what God wants us to do when we are mistreated by others.

Jesus Was Falsely Charged With Blasphemy

Eventually, a religious trial took place that night in Caiaphas' palace, and the religious leaders looked for people who would falsely testify against Jesus so they could put Him to death, but they couldn't find anyone (*see* Matthew 26:57-60).

Again and again, they brought charges against Him. Matthew 26:63 says, "But Jesus held his peace, and the high priest answered and said unto him, I adjure thee by the living God, that thou tell us whether thou be the Christ, the Son of God."

To this, Jesus replied, "…Thou hast said: nevertheless I say unto you, Hereafter shall ye see the Son of man sitting on the right hand of power, and coming in the clouds of heaven. Then the high priest rent his clothes, saying, He hath spoken blasphemy; what further need have we of witnesses? Behold, now ye have heard his blasphemy" (Matthew 26:64,65).

There you have it. The religious leaders who took part in this illegal trial charged Jesus with the crime of blasphemy because He declared Himself the Son of God.

All the Religious Leaders *Spit* in Jesus' Face

At that point, Caiaphas and his entourage began to do the unthinkable! The Bible says:

> **Then did they spit in his face, and buffeted him; and others smote him with the palms of their hands, saying, Prophesy unto us, thou Christ, Who is he that smote thee?**
> **— Matthew 26:67,68**

Notice the passage says, "Then did THEY spit in His face." The Greek word for "they" refers to *all the scribes and elders* who were assembled for the meeting that night, which historically was about 100 people. One by one, each of these so-called spiritual leaders who were clothed in their religious garments walked up to Jesus and spit in His face!

Spitting in someone's face during that time was considered to be the strongest thing you could do to show utter disgust, repugnance, dislike, or hatred. When someone spattered his spit on another person's face, that spit was meant to humiliate, demean, debase, and shame that person. To make it worse, the one spitting would get close to the other person's face and spit as hard as he could to make it even more humiliating.

By the time these 100 religious leaders had finished taking turns spitting on Jesus, their spit was dripping down from His forehead into His eyes, dribbling down His nose, His cheekbones, and His chin, and even oozing down onto His clothes. And remember, the men acting so hatefully were religious leaders!

What makes this entire scene even more shocking is that Malchus — the servant of Caiaphas whom Jesus had just healed in the Garden of Gethsemane — was in all probability standing at the side of Caiaphas, watching all this happen, and even participating in this horrific behavior.

Jesus Was Also Repeatedly *Punched* and *Slapped*

But these warped religious leaders didn't stop there. After they grew tired of spitting on Jesus, they doubled up their fists and one by one they hit Him violently in the face. Matthew records what unfolded, saying:

> **Then did they spit in his face, and buffeted him; and others smote him with the palms of their hands, saying, Prophesy unto us, thou Christ, Who is he that smote thee?**
> **— Matthew 26:67,68**

The word "buffeted" here means *to strike with the fist* and pictures a person who is *violently beaten*. Moreover, this passage says the religious leaders also "smote Him with the palms of their hands." Not only was this brutal — it was sadistic! Humiliating Jesus with their spit and curses didn't satisfy the hatred of these men, so their fists and their palms became their weapons of abuse.

Every time they spit on Him, they were spitting on the anointing on His life.

Every time they struck Him, they were leveling a punch against the anointing.

These religious leaders were so proud and so paranoid about Jesus getting more attention than themselves that they simply wanted to destroy Him. They hated Jesus and the anointing that operated through Him to such an extent that they voted to have Him executed.

The Temple Police Also Abused and Mocked Jesus

When we turn to Luke's gospel, we discover additional details about what happened to Jesus during His phony trial. Luke 22:63 tells us,

And the men that held Jesus mocked him, and smote him.

Notice it says the "men that held Jesus." This specifically refers to the *temple guards* who were working with Caiaphas and holding Jesus while the religious leaders deliberated. So along with the 100 Jewish leaders who spit on, punched, and slapped Jesus, here we find that the temple guards who brought Jesus into in custody also joined in the brutal treatment of Him.

First, it says they "mocked" Him. In Greek, this is the word *empaidzo*, and it depicts *playing a game with children* or *amusing a crowd by impersonating someone in a silly and exaggerated way.* For instance, this word could be used to depict a game of charades when someone intends to comically portray someone or even make fun of someone. The use of this word *empaidzo* tells us that these guards mimicked and impersonated Jesus that night, turning a few minutes of that nightmarish night into a stage of comedy at Jesus' expense.

They put on quite a show, pretending to be Jesus as He was ministering to people. Perhaps they laid hands on each other as if they were healing the sick, or they pretended to be the people Jesus ministered to. It's possible that they laid on the floor and quivered, as if they were being liberated from devils, or they acted as if they had been blind but now could suddenly see. It was all a big game of charades to make fun of Jesus.

Luke 22:63 goes on to say that these temple police officers "smote Him," and the word "smote" is the Greek word *dero*, which describes *the grueling and barbaric practice of beating a slave.* This word was so dreadful that it is often translated *to flay*, such as *to flay the flesh from an animal or human being.* Thus, the temple police literally beat Jesus like one would have beaten a slave.

The Jewish Leaders Continued the Sadistic Games

At that point, it appears that the religious leaders reentered the scene and picked up where the temple police left off. Caiaphas and his religious mafia then initiated the next level of abuse, which we read about in Luke 22:64:

And when they had blindfolded him, they struck him on the face, and asked him, saying, Prophesy, who is it that smote thee?

The Greek word for "blindfolded" means *to wrap a veil or garment about someone, thus hiding his eyes so he can't see.* Just as the guards played charades at Jesus' expense, now Caiaphas and the scribes and Pharisees decided to play blind man's bluff! Once Jesus was blindfolded, "…They struck him on the face, and asked him, saying, Prophesy, who is it that smote thee?" (Luke 22:64)

The word "struck" is the Greek word *paio*, which describes *a strike that stings* and indicates they *slapped* Jesus on the face repeatedly. After each slap or two, the scribes and elders sadistically badgered Jesus, saying things like, "Come on, prophet! If You're so good at prophesying and knowing things supernaturally, tell us which one of us just slapped You!"

They Blasphemously Spoke to Jesus

When the religious mob tired of playing games, they began to speak blasphemously to Jesus. Luke 22:65 says, "And many other things blasphemously spake they against him." In the original Greek, the word for "blasphemously" here means *to accuse; to speak against; to slander;* or *to speak derogatory words for the purpose of injuring or harming one's reputation.* This word signifies *profane, foul, and unclean language.*

Once these religious leaders "took off the lid," every foul thing that was hiding inside them came to the surface. It was as if a monster had been let out, and they couldn't get it back in its cage! Just imagine — a gathering of 100 top religious leaders, dressed in their regal robes and sashes, all crowded around Jesus, punching Him, slapping Him, spitting in His face, and screaming blasphemous words.

This vivid picture was a confirmation of what Jesus had told these Jewish higher-ups earlier: "Woe unto you, scribes and Pharisees, hypocrites! For ye are like unto whited sepulchres, which indeed appear beautiful outward, but are within full of dead men's bones, and of all uncleaness" (Matthew 23:27).

If the people of Israel had been allowed to peek into that room that night, they would have been shocked to see their supposedly godly leaders slapping Jesus, spitting on Him, punching Him with their fists, and then screaming words of profanity right in His face! Although they may have put on a great act in public, inwardly they were so rotten that they could not hide their true nature anymore.

Commit Yourself Into God's Hands

Friend, if you ever find yourself in a predicament similar to the one Jesus faced, where you are being unjustly treated and people are emotionally abusing you or taking advantage of you, and there's nothing you can do to defend yourself, commit yourself into God's hands.

Out loud or in your heart, say, "Father, I'm committing myself into Your care. I ask You to defend me and that Your resurrection power will flow through me. In Jesus' name, Amen."

God is fair and just. He sees absolutely everything and always judges righteously. When you cry out to Him, He will give you the wisdom to know when you should speak, when you should be quiet, and exactly what steps you must take.

STUDY QUESTIONS

Study to shew thyself approved unto God, a workman that needeth not to be ashamed, rightly dividing the word of truth.
— 2 Timothy 2:15

1. In this lesson, we see that Jesus was first brought to the palace of Caiaphas, the high priest, and then handed off to the temple police, being brutally assaulted and abused repeatedly from about 100 religious leaders and then again by the temple officers. How do all the details of what Jesus went through affect the way you see Him and what He did for you?

2. One of the most vital truths for you to know as a believer is that *Jesus never sinned.* This foundational fact is confirmed in Second Corinthians 5:21; Hebrews 4:15; 7:26; 9:14; First Peter 1:18,19; 2:22; and First John 3:5. Take time to reflect on these verses and ask the Holy Spirit to make this truth real and personally relevant in your life.

PRACTICAL APPLICATION

But be ye doers of the word, and not hearers only,
deceiving your own selves.
—James 1:22

1. Have you ever been severely mistreated or abused? Are you experiencing unjust treatment right now? If so, get alone with the Lord and begin to pour out your heart to Him in prayer (*see* Psalm 62:8). He will listen, He will strengthen and heal you, and He will show you what to do.

2. The Bible specifically says, "Because God's children are human beings — made of flesh and blood — the Son [Jesus] also became flesh and blood..." (Hebrews 2:14 *NLT*). In all respects, Jesus became one of us, being tempted and tested and experiencing all the feelings we do. Take time to meditate on Hebrews 2:14-18 and 4:14-16 in a few Bible versions, including the *Amplified Classic*. (Also consider Philippians 2:5-11.) How do these passages encourage you to more earnestly pray and invite Jesus into every situation you're facing?

LESSON 6

TOPIC

Pilate Looks for a Loophole

SCRIPTURES

1. **Luke 23:2** — And they began to accuse him, saying, We found this fellow perverting the nation, and forbidding to give tribute to Caesar, saying that he himself is Christ a King.

2. **Matthew 27:2** — And when they had bound him, they led him away, and delivered him to Pontius Pilate the governor.

3. **Isaiah 53:7** — He was oppressed, and he was afflicted, yet he opened not his mouth: he is brought as a lamb to the slaughter, and as a sheep before her shearers is dumb, so he openeth not his mouth.

4. **Matthew 27:11** — And Jesus stood before the governor: and the governor asked him, saying, Art thou the King of the Jews? And Jesus said unto him, Thou sayest.

5. **Matthew 27:12** — And when he was accused of the chief priests and elders, he answered nothing.

6. **Matthew 27:13,14** — Then said Pilate unto him, Hearest thou not how many things they witness against thee? And he answered him to never a word; insomuch that the governor marvelled greatly.

7. **Luke 23:3** — Art thou the King of the Jews? And he [Jesus] answered him and said, Thou sayest it.

8. **John 18:36** — My kingdom is not of this world: if my kingdom were of this world, then would my servants fight, that I should not be delivered to the Jews: but now is my kingdom not from hence.

9. **Luke 23:4** — Then said Pilate to the chief priests and to the people, I find no fault in this man.

10. **John 19:12** — And from thenceforth Pilate sought to release him...

11. **Luke 23:8** — And when Herod saw Jesus, he was exceeding glad: for he was desirous to see him of a long season, because he had heard many things of him; and he hoped to have seen some miracle done by him.

12. **Hebrews 4:15,16** — For we have not an high priest which cannot be touched with the feeling of our infirmities; but was in all points tempted like as we are, yet without sin. Let us therefore come boldly unto the throne of grace, that we may obtain mercy, and find grace to help in time of need.

GREEK WORDS

1. "bound" (*desantes*) — the binding, tying up, or securing of an animal

2. "led him away" (*apago*) — a shepherd who ties a rope around the neck of his sheep and then leads it down the path to where it needs to go

3. "marveled greatly" (*thaumadzo*) — to wonder; to be at a loss of words; or to be shocked and amazed

4. "fault" (*aitios*) — no causable, legal reason to prosecute

SYNOPSIS

Have you ever found yourself in a situation that was so difficult that no potential decision seemed like a good option? That is where Pontius Pilate found himself when Jesus of Nazareth was brought into his court. Being an expert in Roman law, he determined that there was no cause to condemn Jesus, but letting Him go would put Pilate in trouble with Roman authorities. Desperate for a way out, he searched for a legal loophole through which he could escape.

The emphasis of this lesson:

Pontius Pilate was a ruthless governor in Judea for ten years and presided over Jesus' trial. Although Jesus was given three chances to defend Himself, He remained silent. Finding no fault in Jesus, Pilate wanted to set Him free. But when he learned that Jesus was from Galilee, a region overseen by Herod, Pilate saw an opportunity to "wash his hands" of his responsibility and sent Jesus there to be dealt with by Herod.

People Were Paranoid About Losing Their Power

In First Century Israel, the land was filled with leaders who were obsessed with holding on to the reins of power, and this paranoia was so epidemic that it had spread to both the religious and political world.

The Jewish religious leadership was certainly paranoid that someone would take their power. The high priest along with the Jewish scribes and elders were suspicious and paranoid of anyone who appeared to be growing in popularity, which is why they didn't like Jesus and the tremendous following He amassed.

Likewise, the political leaders installed by Rome were constantly looking into every nook and cranny to weed out any opponents who were trying to grab hold of their power. The fact is few political leaders from Rome held power for long. Those who remained in power did it by using cruelty and brutality. This leads us to Pontius Pilate, a remarkable governor who had surprising longevity in Judea.

Who Was Pontius Pilate?

Most Roman governors served 12 to 36 months because leadership was constantly changing hands. This was not so with Pilate. He governed Judea for ten years. In fact, he was governor throughout the entire length of Jesus' ministry.

Noted historian Flavius Josephus, who lived in the First Century, wrote that Pilate was ruthless, unsympathetic, and an overall cruel leader who was always putting down plots against him. He was viewed as the supreme authority in all legal matters. As an expert in Roman law, he had the final say-so in nearly all the legal decisions for the territory of Judea.

Though Pilate held this legal power in his hands, he dreaded cases having to do with religion and often permitted such cases to be passed onto the court of the Sanhedrin, over which Caiaphas the high priest presided.

Pilate knew how to play the political game, which is a big reason he managed to stay in power for an entire decade. At the same time, the Jewish leaders also knew how to play political games. For example, they were aware that many complaints had been filed in Rome about Pilate's ruthless style of leadership, and a threat of additional complaints being sent to Rome was often all the Jews needed to manipulate Pilate into doing their bidding.

No doubt this affected Pilate's ultimate decision to crucify Jesus. When the religious mob insisted Jesus be crucified, Pilate wanted to know the reason for their demand, and this is how they answered him:

> **…We found this fellow perverting the nation, and forbidding to give tribute to Caesar, saying that he himself is Christ a King.**
>
> — Luke 23:2

The truth is, the Jewish leaders were jealous of Jesus, which Pilate knew, but they also despised Pilate for his cruelty. The charges brought against Jesus put Pilate in a very bad position politically.

What if news reached Rome that Jesus had perverted the nation, teaching the people to withhold their taxes? Or that Jesus had claimed to be a counter King in place of the Roman emperor? It would be political suicide for Pilate to do nothing about that kind of situation.

Jesus Was 'Led Away' Like an Animal

After the Jewish elders and temple police had finished their vicious treatment of Jesus, Caiaphas gave the word to take Him to Pilate. The Bible says, "And when they had bound him, they led him away, and delivered him to Pontius Pilate the governor" (Matthew 27:2).

The Greek word for "bound" here indicates *the binding, tying up, or securing of an animal.* Likewise, the Greek phrase for "led him away" describes *a shepherd who ties a rope around the neck of his sheep and then leads it down the path to where it needs to go.* Here again, we find the fulfillment of Isaiah 53:7, which says:

He was oppressed, and he was afflicted, yet he opened not his mouth: he is brought as a lamb to the slaughter, and as a sheep before her shearers is dumb, so he openeth not his mouth.

Thus, when they wrapped a rope around Jesus' neck and led Him like a lamb to Pontius Pilate, it was the beginning of His "slaughter." This would be the first round of interrogation Jesus would experience with Pilate.

Matthew 27:11 says, "And Jesus stood before the governor: and the governor asked him, saying, Art thou the King of the Jews? And Jesus said unto him, Thou sayest." Here we see that when Pilate asked a direct question, Jesus refused to directly answer him. Instead, He basically told Pilate, "That's what you say about Me."

Pilate 'Marveled Greatly' at Jesus' Silence

The Scripture goes on to say, "And when he was accused of the chief priests and elders, he answered nothing" (Matthew 27:12). So here, for a second time, Jesus refused to answer or refute the charges that were brought up against Him.

Matthew 27:13 and 14 continues by saying, "Then said Pilate unto him, Hearest thou not how many things they witness against thee? And he answered him to never a word; insomuch that the governor marvelled greatly."

The words "marvelled greatly" in the original Greek mean *to wonder, to be at a loss for words*, or *to be shocked and amazed.* The reason Pilate was amazed is because Roman law permitted prisoners three chances to open their mouths to defend themselves. If a prisoner passed up those three chances to speak in his own defense, it meant he would be automatically charged as "guilty."

A careful look at the text reveals that Jesus passed up all three chances to defend Himself:

In Matthew 27:11, Jesus passed up His *first* chance.

In Matthew 27:12, He passed up His *second* chance.

And in Matthew 27:14, Jesus passed up His *third and final* chance.

Greatly puzzled by Jesus' silence, Pilate asked Him plainly, "Art thou the King of the Jews? And he [Jesus] answered him and said, Thou sayest it" (Luke 23:3). In John's gospel, this interrogation is expanded and includes an additional response from Jesus. He said, "…My kingdom is not of this world: if my kingdom were of this world, then would my servants fight, that I should not be delivered to the Jews: but now is my kingdom not from hence" (John 18:36).

There Was No 'Fault' To Be Found in Jesus

After hearing these answers from Jesus, "then said Pilate to the chief priests and to the people, I find no fault in this man" (Luke 23:4). The word "fault" here means *no causable, legal reason to prosecute*. John 19:12 tells us that at that point in the proceedings, "…from thenceforth Pilate sought to release him…."

Remember, Pilate was the highest legal authority in the land, and no one knew the law better than him. So for Pilate to conclude that there was *no causable, legal reason to prosecute* was significant. Clearly, he didn't want to crucify Jesus, so the Roman governor began looking for a loophole to escape putting this Man to death.

This moved the vicious religious vipers to dig in their heels and devise a scheme that was sure to either get rid of Jesus or get rid of Pilate. Their aim was to see one of three things happen:

1. See Jesus judged by the Roman court, thus ruining His reputation and guaranteeing His crucifixion, while at the same time vindicating themselves in the eyes of the people.

2. See Pilate removed from power on the charge that he was unfaithful to the Roman emperor because he would not crucify a man who claimed to be a rival king to the emperor.

3. Or, if Pilate would not crucify Jesus, they intended to take Jesus back into their own court in the Sanhedrin, where they had the religious authority to stone Him to death for claiming to be the Son of God.

If Pilate would have swiftly given the order for Jesus to be crucified, this political game would have been quickly finished. Then he would have happy Jewish elders on his hands with no charges of treason leveled against him in Rome. This would have also strengthened his ties to the religious community, and he would have been guaranteed to remain in power.

But from the moment Pilate met Jesus, something inside him could not bring him to prosecute Jesus. That is why he gave Christ three opportunities to speak up in His own defense. But Jesus passed on every one of them. Again, this was the fulfillment of Isaiah 53:7, which was written more than 700 years earlier:

> **He was oppressed, and he was afflicted, yet he opened not his mouth: he is brought as a lamb to the slaughter, and as a sheep before her shearers is dumb, so he openeth not his mouth.**

According to Roman law, Jesus should have automatically been declared "guilty" because He passed up His three chances to defend Himself. But Pilate was still searching for a way out of this dilemma.

Pilate Found a Legal Loophole

Pilate's diligence paid off, because as soon as he told the chief priests and Pharisees that he found no fault with Jesus, he learned that Jesus was from Galilee, which made Him the subject of Herod Antipas. It just so happened that Herod was nearby, staying on the other side of town at the old palace of his late father, Herod the Great. He was in Jerusalem to celebrate the Passover with the Jews.

Discovering that Jesus was from Galilee was the legal loophole Pilate longed for! That shifted the full weight of the decision of what to do with Jesus to Herod, because Galilee was Herod's jurisdiction. Accordingly, Pilate ordered Jesus to be transferred to where Herod was staying.

What was Herod's response to all this? Luke 23:8 tells us:

> **And when Herod saw Jesus, he was exceeding glad: for he was desirous to see him of a long season, because he had heard many things of him; and he hoped to have seen some miracle done by him.**

Nevertheless, as we will see in our next lesson, it didn't take long before Herod lost his temper and sent Jesus back to Pilate!

Jesus Was Born To Be the Lamb of God

Jesus surrendered Himself to human authorities and allowed them to wrap a rope around His neck and lead Him like a sheep to His own slaughter. In just a matter of a few hours, Jesus had been brutally abused and blasphemed by Israel's high priest and religious leaders and then assaulted and ridiculed by the temple police. After He was spit on, slapped, punched in the face, blindfolded, and mocked, Caiaphas then shipped Him off to stand trial before Pontius Pilate.

Finding no fault with Jesus, Pilate attempted three times to give Him the opportunity to speak in His own defense, asking Jesus who He was and what He had done to cause the religious leaders to call for His death. But as a lamb is silent before its shearers, Jesus didn't open His mouth.

When Pilate learned that Jesus was a Galilean, he shipped Jesus off to Herod Antipas, who was the recognized authority over that region. But when Jesus remained silent and would not perform miracles at Herod's request, Herod shipped Him back to Pilate again.

Why did Jesus remain silent and refuse to defend Himself? Because He knew who He was, and He knew He was right where He was supposed to be. Jesus was born to be the Lamb of God that would die on the Cross to take away the sins of the world, and the Father empowered Him to fulfill His mission.

Jesus Fully Understands the Troubles You Face

If you have ever been knocked around and passed from one authority figure to another at home, at church, in the workplace, or in the governmental system, you can talk to Jesus about it because He fully understands the predicament you are in now. The Bible confirms this truth, telling us plainly:

> **For we have not an high priest which cannot be touched with the feeling of our infirmities; but was in all points tempted like as we are, yet without sin. Let us therefore come boldly unto the throne of grace, that we may obtain mercy, and find grace to help in time of need.**
> **— Hebrews 4:15,16**

Jesus completely understands the problem you're facing, and you can speak freely to Him about all the emotional ups and downs you feel as a result of your situation. As you come to Him in prayer, know that His throne is a throne of grace — a place where you can obtain mercy and find real mental, emotional, and spiritual strength (*grace*) to help in your time of need.

Regardless of the difficulties you're going through, if you know you are in the will of God, you will make it through! Stay on track, receive God's grace daily, and He will give you a fresh infilling of the Holy Spirit to energize and invigorate you with what you need to remain faithful all the way to the end.

STUDY QUESTIONS

Study to shew thyself approved unto God, a workman that needeth not to be ashamed, rightly dividing the word of truth.
— 2 Timothy 2:15

1. Isaiah 53 was written more than 700 years before the time of Christ, yet it predicts with pinpoint accuracy many of the things Jesus would suffer. Take time to reflect on this chapter and note how it compares to what the gospel writers recorded. How does the fulfillment of what Isaiah wrote encourage you to trust God's Word?

2. Hebrews 4:16 urges us to come boldly to God's throne in prayer and receive His *grace*. According to James 4:6; First Peter 5:5; and Proverbs 3:34, what is the one condition to receiving grace from God when you ask for it?

PRACTICAL APPLICATION

But be ye doers of the word, and not hearers only, deceiving your own selves.
— James 1:22

1. What new details did you learn about Pontius Pilate and his ten-year rule in Judea? Were you aware of the political tension between him and the Jewish leaders? How about his fears over additional complaints sent to Rome?

2. Although God's grace is not something tangible that you can touch or purchase in a store, it is still very real and powerful. Take time to meditate on these verses about God's grace and write down what the Holy Spirit speaks to your heart.

    For the Lord God is a sun and shield; the Lord will give grace and glory; no good thing will He withhold from those who walk uprightly.
    — **Psalm 84:11** (*NKJV*)

    And God is able to make all grace (every favor and earthly blessing) come to you in abundance, so that you may always and under all circumstances and whatever the need be self-sufficient [possessing enough to require no aid or support and furnished in abundance for every good work and charitable donation].
    — **2 Corinthians 9:8** (*AMPC*)

    But He gives us more and more grace (power of the Holy Spirit, to meet this evil tendency and all others fully). That is why He says, God sets Himself against the proud and haughty, but gives grace [continually] to the lowly (those who are humble enough to receive it).
    — **James 4:6** (*AMPC*)

LESSON 7

TOPIC

Herod Finally Meets Jesus

SCRIPTURES

1. **Luke 23:8** — And when Herod saw Jesus, he was exceeding glad: for he was desirous to see him of a long season, because he had heard many things of him; and he hoped to have seen some miracle done by him.

2. **Luke 23:10** — And the chief priests and scribes stood and vehemently accused him.

3. **Luke 23:11** — And Herod with his men of war set him at nought, and mocked him, and arrayed him in a gorgeous robe, and sent him again to Pilate.

4. **Luke 23:14-16** — …Ye have brought this man unto me, as one that perverteth the people: and, behold, I, having examined him before you, have found no fault in this man touching those things whereof ye accuse him: No, nor yet Herod: for I sent you to him; and, lo, nothing worthy of death is done unto him. I will therefore chastise him, and release him.

5. **Luke 23:20,21**— Pilate therefore, willing to release Jesus, spake again to them. But they cried, saying, Crucify him, crucify him.

6. **Luke 23:22** — And he said unto them the third time, Why, what evil hath he done? I have found no cause of death in him: I will therefore chastise him, and let him go.

7. **Luke 22:23** — And they were instant with loud voices, requiring that he might be crucified. And the voices of them and of the chief priests prevailed.

8. **John 19:12** — And from thenceforth Pilate sought to release him: but the Jews cried out, saying, If thou let this man go, thou art not Caesar's friend: whosoever maketh himself a king speaketh against Caesar.

9. **Matthew 27:24** — When Pilate saw that he could prevail nothing, but that rather a tumult was made, he took water, and washed his hands before the multitude, saying, I am innocent of the blood of this just person: see ye to it.

GREEK WORDS

1. "Antipas" — one who is against everything and everyone

2. "saw" (*horao*) — to see; to behold; to delightfully view; to look at with scrutiny; or to look at with the intent to examine

3. "exceeding glad" (*echari lian*) — great; exceedingly great; much; extreme excitement; someone who is ecstatic about something

4. "a long season" (*ek hikanos chronos*) — for many years; for a long time

5. "miracle" (*semeion*) — a sign, a mark, or a token that verifies or authenticates a report; used in the gospels primarily to depict miracles and supernatural events, which means the purpose of such miracles and supernatural events is to verify and authenticate the message of the Gospel

6. "vehemently" (*eutonos*) — at full pitch; at full volume; strenuously or vigorously

7. "men of war" (*strateuma*) — a small detachment of soldiers who were Herod's personal bodyguards

8. "set him at nought" (*exoutheneo*) — to make one out to be nothing; to make light of; to belittle; to disdain; to disregard; to despise; or to treat with maliciousness and contempt

9. "mocked" *(empaidzo)* — to play a game; often used for playing a game with children or to amuse a crowd by impersonating someone in a silly and exaggerated way; used in a game of charades when someone intends to comically portray or even make fun of someone

10. "arrayed" (*periballo*) — to throw about or to drape about, as to drape around one's shoulders

11. "gorgeous robe" (*esthes*) — a robe that is resplendent, glistening, or magnificent; frequently used to depict a garment made of sumptuous, brightly colored materials

12. "cried" (*epiphoneo*) — to shout, to scream, to yell, to shriek, or to screech; the tense means they were hysterically screaming and shrieking at the top of their voices — totally out of control and without pause

13. "they were instant" (*epikeima*) — to pile evidence on top of Pilate, nearly burying him in reasons why Jesus had to be crucified

SYNOPSIS

Pontius Pilate loathed having to deal with religious issues involving the Jews. Yet, suddenly, he found himself swept into a bitter brawl with Caiaphas and the Jewish leaders over a man called Jesus of Nazareth. Why did the chief priests and scribes vehemently demand Jesus' death? Their jealousy concerning His popularity was no reason for Pilate to consent to His execution. If there was any way to escape having to deal with Jesus, Pilate wanted it.

Then he discovered that Jesus was from Galilee, which was under the jurisdiction of Herod Antipas. So without hesitation, Pilate took advantage of this legal loophole and sent Jesus off to Herod, who happened to be in Jerusalem for the Passover, staying at the palace of his late father. Finally, Herod would get to meet Jesus face to face, but his joy would certainly be short-lived.

The emphasis of this lesson:

Herod Antipas ruled the region of Galilee from where Jesus had come. He had heard stories of Jesus all his life and was thrilled at the chance of meeting Him. But when Jesus would not perform a miracle, Herod became furious. He and his soldiers mocked Jesus and then sent Him back to Pilate.

Who Was Herod Antipas?

There were several men named Herod who ruled in biblical times. The first and most famous was "Herod the Great" who was made the first governor of Galilee when he was 25 years old. He had several sons, some of which he killed due to his paranoia that they were trying to steal his throne. Nevertheless, three sons survived and ruled after him, and one of them was Herod Antipas.

The region of Galilee and Peraea, located on the east bank of the Jordan, was assigned to Herod Antipas. What is interesting to note is that the name "Antipas" is a compound of two Greek words: the word *anti*, which means *against*, and the word *pas*, which is *all-inclusive* and describes *everyone*. Hence the name "Antipas" means *one who is against everything and everyone*.

This name alone should tell us something about Herod's personality. He was a very divisive man known for his trickery and deviousness. Even Jesus compared Herod Antipas to a *fox* — an animal considered to be the epitome of trickery and that was usually unclean and infected with sickness.

When Jesus called Herod a fox, it was the equivalent of saying *Herod was a sneaky, lying, deceiving, dishonest, infected, sick individual.* If you study the ministry of Jesus, you will find that He never used derogatory words to describe political leaders. Calling Herod Antipas a fox was the closest Jesus ever came to saying something negative about a political leader.

Keep in mind, Jesus was from Galilee, and Herod Antipas lived in Galilee. Specifically, Herod lived in Sepphoris, the city just a few miles northwest of Nazareth where Jesus' grandparents lived and His father, Joseph, had worked as a carpenter. Sepphoris was the thriving city Jesus frequently visited. Hence, He saw firsthand the behavior and activities of Herod Antipas.

Herod Was Jubilant To Meet Jesus

Upon the orders of Pontius Pilate, Jesus was taken to Herod Antipas, "and when Herod saw Jesus, he was exceeding glad: for he was desirous to see him of a long season, because he had heard many things of him; and he hoped to have seen some miracle done by him" (Luke 23:8).

In this verse, the word "saw" in Greek means *to see; to behold;* or *to delightfully view*. It carries the idea of *looking at something with scrutiny* or *to look at with the intent to examine*. The use of this word tells us that when Herod saw Jesus, he literally looked Him over, scrutinizing and examining every detail of the Man who appeared before him. He was excited and delighted to finally behold the miracle-worker he had heard so much about. This verse confirms the legendary status Jesus had reached in his lifetime.

Scripture says that Herod was "exceeding glad" that He was meeting Jesus, which in the original Greek means *great; exceedingly great; or much excitement*. It depicts *extreme excitement* or *someone who is ecstatic about something*. Indeed, Herod was nearly jumping up and down on the inside! The Jesus he had heard about for so long was now standing in front of him.

Even Herod longed for a chance to see Jesus and to experience His miracles! That is why Luke 23:8 says, "…He was desirous to see him of a long season, because he had heard many things of him…." Notice the phrase "a long season." In Greek, this means *for many years* or *for a long time*. Again, this should tell us how well-known Jesus had become during His ministry and how He was a legend even in the Herod family.

The name *Jesus* was one the Herod household had heard for many years! Herod Antipas and his brothers had heard many tales about Jesus' supernatural birth, including that the magi from the east had come to worship Him. They had learned of the attempts of their father (King Herod the Great) to kill Jesus by ordering all the babies in Bethlehem to be murdered. Likewise, they had discovered how Jesus and His parents had slipped into Egypt and waited for the right moment to come back into Israel.

The ministry of Jesus had been touching the nation with healing and delivering power, and now Jesus Himself was standing in Herod's presence! Herod was most excited to meet Jesus because "…he hoped to have seen some miracle done by him" (Luke 23:8). The Greek word for "miracle" in this verse is the word for *a sign, a mark,* or *a token that verifies or authenticates a report.* It is used in the gospels primarily to depict miracles and supernatural events, which means the purpose of such miracles and supernatural events is to verify and authenticate the message of the Gospel.

Jesus Was Accused and Mocked

Jesus was known for having a ministry that was overflowing with miracles, and Herod wanted to personally see a miracle performed by Jesus! But when Herod questioned Jesus, He didn't utter a word, much less perform a miracle (*see* Luke 23:9). This enraged the chief priests and scribes who stood by Jesus and began to vehemently accuse him. They had accompanied Jesus from Pilate's palace to Herod's residence and were so furious that they began screaming and yelling uncontrollably.

The word "vehemently" in Luke 23:10 is a Greek word that means *at full pitch; at full volume; strenuously;* or *vigorously*, which means these chief priests and scribes began "screaming their heads off," saying things like, "Some miracle-worker You are! You have no power! You're a fraud! If You can work miracles, why don't You work one right now! You're nothing but a charlatan!"

As rage began to escalate, Herod and his "men of war" stepped in and joined the verbal annihilation of Jesus. The Bible says, "And Herod with his men of war set him at nought, and mocked him, and arrayed him in a gorgeous robe, and sent him again to Pilate" (Luke 23:11).

The phrase "men of war" in the Greek text describes *a small detachment of soldiers who were Herod's personal bodyguards.* Although Herod was a low-level king, he and his bodyguards were supposed to function with dignity, but here we see their actions were quite atrocious. Specifically, the Bible says that these bodyguards "set him [Jesus] at nought," which in the original Greek text means *to make one out to be nothing; to make light of; to belittle; to disdain; to disregard; to despise;* or *to treat with maliciousness and contempt.* That is how they treated Jesus.

Along with disregarding, distaining, and belittling Jesus as if He was nothing, Herod's bodyguards also "mocked" Him. This word "mocked" is the Greek word *empaidzo*, the same word we saw in Luke 22:63, describing how the temple police *played games* with Jesus while they held Him in custody.

This word *empaidzo* is often used for *playing a game with children* or *to amuse a crowd by impersonating someone in a silly and exaggerated way*. It was used to depict a game of charades when someone intended to comically portray or even make fun of someone. Hence, Herod Antipas, a low-level king, along with his bodyguards, began to mockingly impersonate Jesus!

They "hammed it up," turning that moment into a comedy of errors. No doubt, they pretended as if they were healing the sick or that they were the ones in need, lying on the floor and quivering as if they were being liberated from devils, or acting as if they were blind and then suddenly able to see. It was all a game of charades intended to mimic and make fun of Jesus.

Then "…[They] arrayed him in a gorgeous robe, and sent him again to Pilate" (Luke 23:11). In Greek, the word for "arrayed" means *to throw about*, or *to drape about*, as *to drape around one's shoulders*. And the words "gorgeous robe" picture *a robe that is resplendent, glistening*, or *magnificent*. This term was frequently used to depict *a garment made of sumptuous, brightly colored materials*. In all likelihood, this was a garment that had been previously worn by a politician! When candidates were running for public office, they wore beautiful, brightly colored clothes just like this.

Jesus Was Returned to Pilate's Court

When Herod and his bodyguards were done playing games with Jesus, they "…arrayed him in a gorgeous robe, and sent him again to Pilate" (Luke 23:11). Herod's treatment of Jesus was the equivalent of saying, "This is no king! He's only another candidate — a pretender who thinks he's running for some kind of office!" That was the purpose of throwing the brightly colored robe on Jesus.

With Jesus being returned to Pilate's court, Pilate was now forced to deal with Jesus and the pressure put on him by the chief priests and elders. The Bible says,

> **And Pilate, when he had called together the chief priests and the rulers and the people, said unto them, Ye have brought this man unto me, as one that perverteth the people: and, behold, I, having examined him before you, have found no fault in this man touching those things whereof ye accuse him: No, nor yet**

Herod: for I sent you to him; and, lo, nothing worthy of death is done unto him. I will therefore chastise him, and release him.
— Luke 23:13-16

Remember, Pilate was the chief legal authority of the land. He knew Roman law, and from a legal standpoint, he couldn't find a single crime Jesus had committed. To add weight to his decision, Pilate backed his view by essentially saying, "Even Herod has arrived at the same conclusion as I have: this Man has committed no legal offense."

In hopes of appeasing the religious leaders and the mob they had stirred up, Pilate offered to chastise Jesus and then release Him. Besides, it was Roman custom to release one criminal at the time of the Passover feast. But just having Jesus chastised wouldn't be enough to satisfy the bloody appetite of the religious mob.

'Crucify Him!'

Luke 23:18 and 19 says, "And they cried out all at once, saying, Away with this man, and release unto us Barabbas: (Who for a certain sedition made in the city, and for murder, was cast into prison.). At this point, Pilate was both frustrated and bewildered. Even though he was ruthless in his dealings, he knew Jesus was innocent of any crime and wanted to set Him free. Scripture says:

Pilate therefore, willing to release Jesus, spake again to them. But they cried, saying, Crucify him, crucify him.
— Luke 23:20,21

The word "cried" here means *to shout*; *to scream*; *to yell*; *to shriek*; or *to screech*, and the tense means they were hysterically screaming and shrieking at the top of their voices — totally out of control and without pause.

For a third time, the Bible says Pilate tried to reason with the religious leaders, saying:

…Why, what evil hath he done? I have found no cause of death in him: I will therefore chastise him, and let him go. And they were instant with loud voices, requiring that he might be crucified. And the voices of them and of the chief priests prevailed.
— Luke 23:22,23

Note the phrase "they were instant." The word "instant" in Greek means *to pile on top of*, and it indicates that these chief priests and elders nearly buried Pilate with reasons on top of reasons as to why Jesus had to be crucified.

John's gospel offers us some details not found elsewhere. In addition to overwhelming Pilate with endless reasons and screaming at him at the top of their lungs, they also threatened him saying, "…If thou let this man go, thou art not Caesar's friend: whosoever maketh himself a king speaketh against Caesar" (John 19:12).

This was the breaking point at which Pilate knew he was in a bad fix. He really didn't want to prosecute Jesus and sentence Him to death, but he knew if he let Jesus go, the Jewish leaders could really stir up trouble for him with Rome.

Pilate Publicly Washed His Hands of the Matter

In that moment, Pilate decided to sacrifice Jesus and save himself. But he first wanted to make it clear to everyone that was watching and listening that he didn't agree with what they were doing. Matthew 27:24 says:

> **When Pilate saw that he could prevail nothing, but that rather a tumult was made, he took water, and washed his hands before the multitude, saying, I am innocent of the blood of this just person: see ye to it.**

Water is a cleansing agent, and in the First Century, it was believed that washing one's hands the way Pilate did was symbolic of washing away or removing one's guilt. So when Pilate washed his hands in that basin of water, it was his public declaration, "I am clear of all guilt regarding the blood of this just person!"

Sadly, when faced with the choice of enforcing the truth or sacrificing his career, Pilate caved to the insurmountable cries of the religious leaders and sacrificed Jesus. He ignored his conscience to save himself, giving the order for Jesus to be scourged and then crucified.

In the next program, we will see what a Roman scourge is and what Jesus endured.

STUDY QUESTIONS

**Study to shew thyself approved unto God, a workman that
needeth not to be ashamed, rightly dividing the word of truth.
— 2 Timothy 2:15**

1. Prior to this lesson, what did you know about Herod Antipas? What new insights did you discover about his name, his character, and his dealings with Jesus at the time of His arrest?

2. Pilate's decision to have Jesus scourged and crucified was to appease the Jews and save his career. According to First Samuel 15:10-31, another well-known ruler disobeyed God for fear of people. Who was it, what did he do, and what happened as a result?

3. Living to please people can be very dangerous, and God warns us about this in Deuteronomy 1:17; Proverbs 29:25; Isaiah 51:11-13; Jeremiah 38:19 and 20; and Luke 12:4 and 5. As you read these verses, what is the Holy Spirit showing you?

PRACTICAL APPLICATION

**But be ye doers of the word, and not hearers only,
deceiving your own selves.
— James 1:22**

1. Herod Antipas and the religious leaders violently took out their frustrations on Jesus when He failed to meet their expectations. Be honest. How do you tend to react when Jesus fails to meet *your* expectations? How does seeing the reaction of these people help you see your own reaction differently?

2. When you read that Pilate found absolutely no fault in Jesus, yet he sentenced Him to death, what does that say to you about Pilate's character? Do you believe that his public handwashing cleared him of the guilt of ordering that Jesus be crucified? Why or why not?

3. No doubt, Pilate gave in to the crowd's demands for fear of losing his position. He went against what he knew in his heart was right — that Jesus was innocent. Is there an area in your life where you are doing this? If so, where? Pray and ask the Holy Spirit to show you the root reason for compromising and what you can do to cooperate with Him and see this change in your life.

TOPIC

The Horror of a Roman Scourging

SCRIPTURES

1. **Matthew 27:26** — …When he [Pilate] had scourged Jesus, he delivered him to be crucified.

2. **Deuteronomy 25:3** — Forty stripes he may give him, and not exceed….

3. **Isaiah 52:14** — As many were astonied at thee; his visage was so marred more than any man, and his form more than the sons of men.

4. **Isaiah 53:5** — But he was wounded for our transgressions, he was bruised for our iniquities: the chastisement of our peace was upon him; and with his stripes we are healed.

5. **1 Peter 2:24** — Who his own self bare our sins in his own body on the tree, that we, being dead to sins, should live unto righteousness: by whose stripes ye were healed.

6. **Matthew 27:27-29** — Then the soldiers of the governor took Jesus into the common hall, and gathered unto him the whole band of soldiers. And they stripped him, and put on him a scarlet robe. And when they had platted a crown of thorns, they put it upon his head, and a reed in his right hand: and they bowed the knee before him, and mocked him, saying, Hail, King of the Jews!

7. **Matthew 27:30** — And they spit upon him, and took the reed, and smote him on the head. And after that they had mocked him, they took the robe off from him, and put his own raiment on him, and led him away to crucify him

8. **Philippians 2:10,11** — That at the name of Jesus every knee should bow, of things in heaven, and things in earth, and things under the earth; and that every tongue should confess that Jesus Christ is Lord, to the glory of God the Father.

GREEK WORDS

1. "scourge" (*phragello*) — one of the most horrific words ever used in the ancient world because of the terrible images that immediately came to mind when a person heard it
2. "stripes" (*molopsi*) — a full-body bruise; a terrible lashing that draws blood and produces discoloration and swelling of the entire body
3. "healed" (*iaomai*) — physical healing; a word borrowed from the medical term to describe the physical healing or curing of the human body
4. "band of soldiers" (*spira*) — a cohort; a group of 300 to 600 Roman soldiers
5. "stripped" (*ekduo*) — to totally unclothe or to fully undress; they didn't just strip Him to His underclothes; they stripped Him completely naked
6. "scarlet robe" (*chlamuda kokkinen*) — a robe that has been dyed a deep crimson or scarlet color — the deeply colored crimson and scarlet robes worn by royalty or nobility
7. "put it upon" (*epitithimi*) — they violently pushed or forcefully shoved this crown of thorns onto Jesus' head
8. "crown" (*stephanos*) — a coveted victor's crown
9. "bowed the knee" (*gonupeteo)* — to fall down upon one's knees
10. "smote" (*tupto*) — the soldiers repeatedly struck Jesus again and again on the head

SYNOPSIS

Few things struck terror in the hearts and minds of people in the First Century like the Roman scourge. Jesus endured this lethal beating for you because He loves you and wants you to be healed and whole in all areas of your life. In this lesson, we will fix our eyes on Jesus and examine what He went through. Remember, "When you find yourselves flagging in your faith, go over that story again, item by item, that long litany of hostility he plowed through. That will shoot adrenaline into your souls!" (Hebrews 12:3 *MSG.*)

The emphasis of this lesson:

The Roman scourge Jesus received was a torturous thrashing across His entire body, causing indescribable disfigurement and tremendous blood loss. This potentially lethal beating was followed by even more cruelty

and mocking by the Roman soldiers. The violent abuse He received is beyond what any human could endure. Yet He did it for you and all humanity.

The Column on Which Jesus Was Scourged Can Still Be Seen Today

When visiting the Church of the Holy Sepulchre, most people go to see Jesus' tomb and the ruins of Golgotha, but they fail to see something else very important. Inside that church in Jerusalem are two fragments of stone columns dating to the First Century that are disfigured with the marks caused by a Roman scourge. These are from the time when Pontius Pilate was the governor of Judea.

One column, which is whitish and granite and rests behind a piece of glass, is overseen by the Catholic Church, and they believe it is the actual column on which Jesus was scourged.

If you continue following the circular passageway within the Church of the Holy Sepulchre, you will come to a second column, and it is overseen by the Orthodox Church who claims it is the actual column on which Jesus was scourged. It is a blackish-looking column exhibited high on a shelf in the walls of an interior chapel within the church, and it is also marred by a Roman scourging. It is actually a fragment of two pieces, and the other piece of that same blackish column is on display at the Orthodox Church in Istanbul.

Each of these historical churches claim their column is the actual column on which Jesus was scourged before He carried the cross to be crucified at Golgotha. When you see these columns and the marks that were made on the granite by the scourge, it makes you wonder, *If a scourge would do that to stone, what would it do to a human body?*

The Process of a Roman Scourging

According to Matthew 27:26, "…When he [Pilate] had scourged Jesus, he delivered him to be crucified." The word "scourged" in Greek is one of the most horrific words ever used in the ancient world because of the terrible images that immediately came to mind when a person heard it. Although this is not pleasant to hear, you need to know what Jesus went through to pay the price for our healing.

When a decision was made to scourge an individual, the victim was first stripped completely naked so his entire flesh would be open to the beating action of the torturer's whip. In most illustrations, it shows Jesus with a little garment wrapped around His midsection, but in reality, Jesus was completely naked when He was scourged, allowing the whip to touch every single part of His back.

Once naked, the victim was normally bound to a two-foot-high scourging post made of stone. His hands were tied over his head to a metal ring, and his wrists were securely shackled to that ring to restrain his body from movement. When in this locked position, the victim couldn't wiggle, move, or dodge the lashes that were being laid across his body.

Romans were professionals at scourging and took special delight in the fact that they were the "best" at punishing a victim with this brutal act. Once a victim was harnessed to the post and stretched over it, Roman soldiers put him through unimaginable torture. One writer notes that the mere anticipation of the whipping caused the victim's body to grow rigid, the muscles to knot in his stomach, the color to drain from his cheeks, and his lips to draw tight against his teeth as he waited for the first sadistic blow that would begin tearing his body open.

The scourge itself was a short, wooden handle with several 18- to 24-inch-long straps of leather protruding from it. The ends of these pieces of leather were knotted with sharp pieces of metal, wire, glass, and jagged fragments of bone. This was considered to be one of the most feared and deadly weapons of the Roman world.

The scourging was so ghastly that the mere threat of it could calm a crowd or bend the will of the strongest rebel. Even the most hardened criminal recoiled from the prospect of being submitted to the vicious beating of a Roman scourge.

Most often, two torturers were utilized to carry out this punishment, simultaneously lashing the victim from two sides. As dual whips struck the victim, the leather straps with their sharp, jagged objects descended and extended over his entire back, and each piece of metal, wire, bone, or glass cut deeply through the victim's skin and into his flesh and shredded his muscles and sinews.

Every time the whip pounded across the victim, those straps of leather curled tortuously around his torso, biting painfully and deeply into the skin of his abdomen and upper chest. As each stroke lacerated the sufferer, even if he tried to thrash about, he was unable to move because his wrists were held so firmly to the metal ring on the stone column.

Every time the torturers struck a victim, the straps of leather attached to the wooden handle would cause multiple lashes as the sharp objects at the end of each strap sank into the flesh and then raked across the victim's body. The torturer would then jerk back, pulling hard in order to tear whole pieces of human flesh from the body.

The victim's back, buttocks, back of the legs, stomach, upper chest, and face would soon be disfigured by the slashing blows of the whip. Helpless to escape the whip, victims would scream for mercy that this anguish might come to an end.

What History Recorded About Roman Scourgings

Historical records describe a victim's back as being so mutilated after a Roman scourging that his spine could actually be exposed. Others recorded how the bowels of a victim could actually spill out through the open wounds created by the whip.

The Early Church historian Eusebius wrote: "The veins were laid bare, and the very muscles, sinews, and bowels of the victim were open to exposure."[1]

The Roman torturer would so aggressively strike his victim that he wouldn't even take the time to untangle the bloody, flesh-filled straps as he lashed the whip across the victim's mangled body over and over again. If the scourging wasn't stopped, the slicing of the whip would eventually flay the victim's flesh off his body.

With so many blood vessels sliced open by the whip, the victim would begin to experience a profuse loss of blood and bodily fluids. The heart would pump harder and harder, struggling to get blood to the parts of the body that were bleeding profusely. But it was like pumping water through an open water hydrant; there was nothing to stop the blood from pouring through the victim's open wounds.

This loss of blood caused the victim's blood pressure to drop drastically, and because of the massive loss of bodily fluids, he would experience excruciating thirst, often fainting from the pain and eventually going into shock. Frequently, the victim's heartbeat would become so irregular that he would go into cardiac arrest.

That is a picture of a Roman scourging.

The Difference Between Jewish and Roman Scourgings

According to Scripture, there were two specific scourgings. One was done by the Romans and the other by the Jews. Deuteronomy 25:3 says Jews could give 40 lashes to a victim, but because the fortieth lash usually proved fatal, the number of lashes given was reduced to 39.

When Jesus was scourged, it was by the hands of the Romans, not the Jews. Romans had no limit to the number of lashes they could give a victim, so exactly how many lashes Christ received is not known. Yet the physical effects were devastating.

Although the New Testament doesn't tell us exactly what Jesus looked like after He was scourged, we do have a prophetic description of it in Isaiah 52:14, which says:

> **As many were astonied at thee; his visage was marred more than any man, and his form more than the sons of men.**

This verse prophetically tells us that Jesus' visage, (His face and appearance), and His form were marred more than any other man. He was so disfigured by the Roman scourge that people were astonished at the sight of Him. That is what He went through for us!

By His Stripes We Were Healed

Friend, it was because of those stripes that we are healed. This was first declared by the prophet Isaiah more than 700 years before Christ lived. He wrote:

> **But he was wounded for our transgressions, he was bruised or our iniquities: the chastisement of our peace was upon him; and with his stripes we are healed.**
> **— Isaiah 53:5**

This verse declares that the price for our healing would be paid for by the stripes that were laid across Jesus' back. The apostle Peter echoed this same passage in his first letter, proclaiming:

...By whose stripes ye were healed.

— 1 Peter 2:24

The Greek word for "stripes" here is *molopsai*, and it describes *a full-body bruise; a terrible lashing that draws blood and that produces discoloration and swelling of the entire body.* Jesus' entire body was swollen, discolored, and disfigured by this scourging. And Peter says it was by these stripes we were *healed.*

The Greek word in the original text for "healed" is *iaomai*, and it indicates *physical healing*, not spiritual healing. It is a word borrowed from the medical term to describe *the physical healing or curing of the human body.* This is a promise of bodily healing that belongs to all who have been redeemed and are children of God.

Make no mistake — just as Jesus took our sins when He died on the Cross in our place, He also took our sicknesses and pains on Himself when they laid those lashes across His entire body. His broken body was the payment that guaranteed our physical healing.

Considering what Jesus endured to bear your sicknesses, isn't that enough to convince you how much He wants you to be physically well?

Roman Soldiers Inflicted
Yet Another Round of Abuse

After the scourging, Pilate delivered Jesus to the Roman soldiers. Matthew 27:27-29 says,

> **Then the soldiers of the governor took Jesus into the common hall, and gathered unto him the whole band of soldiers. And they stripped him, and put on him a scarlet robe. And when they had platted a crown of thorns, they put it upon his head, and a reed in his right hand: and they bowed the knee before him, and mocked him, saying, Hail, King of the Jews!**

The phrase "band of soldiers" is translated from the Greek word *speira*, which describes *a Roman cohort of soldiers,* which was *300 to 600*

well-trained soldiers who were equipped with the finest weaponry of the day.
This band of soldiers came together to mock Jesus.

First, they "stripped" Him. The word "stripped" means *to totally unclothe* or *to fully undress*, which tells us they didn't just strip Him to His underclothes; they stripped Him completely naked in front of 300 to 600 soldiers. In that moment, Jesus was so shamed, and He took our shame upon Himself.

Next, the soldiers wrapped Jesus in a "scarlet robe." These words describe *a robe that has been dyed a deep crimson or scarlet color,* and these deeply colored crimson and scarlet robes were worn by royalty or nobility. It's possible that the Roman soldiers pulled an old royal robe from Pilate's closet and brought it to the courtyard to put on Jesus.

Then they "…platted a crown of thorns, they put it upon his head…" (Matthew 27:29). The thorns that grew in that area were long and sharp like nails. The soldiers took vines loaded with these sharp and dangerous thorns, then they carefully wove together those razor-sharp, prickly, jagged vines until they formed a tightly woven, dangerous circle that resembled the shape of a crown.

Matthew 27:29 says, "…They put it upon his head…." The phrase "put it upon" means they *violently pushed* or *forcefully shoved* this crown of thorns onto Jesus' head, and as those thorns scraped across His brow, it ripped His skin free from His skull, and the blood began to pour and pour down His face.

This brings us to the word "crown," which is the Greek word *stephanos*. This word describes *a coveted victor's crown.* What those soldiers did not know is that they were crowning Jesus for the greatest victory of the ages!

The soldiers put "a reed in his right hand" (Matthew 27:29). Interestingly, during that time, there was a beautiful pool in the middle of Pilate's inner courtyard where "reeds" grew. There was also a famous statue called "Ave Caesar," which depicted Caesar holding a staff, or a scepter, in his right hand, being mighty and powerful.

When the soldiers pulled a "reed" from one of the ponds or fountains to put in Jesus' hand, they were, no doubt, dressing Jesus like an emperor, but they were mocking Him as a charlatan emperor.

They mockingly bowed before Jesus. Matthew 27:29 goes on to say that the soldiers also "…bowed the knee before him, and mocked him, saying, Hail, King of the Jews!" The phrase "bowed the knee" literally means *to fall down upon one's knees*. In other words, the soldiers each dropped to their knees as they laughed at and mocked Him.

They spit on Him, took the reed, and smote Him on the head. That is what we read in Matthew 27:30. Each soldier spit right in Jesus' blood-drenched face, and then each soldier grabbed the reed from His hand to strike Him as hard as possible on His already wounded head.

The Greek word for "smote" in this verse depicts the soldiers *repeatedly striking* Jesus again and again on the head, and when they had their fill of their sadistic games, "…They took the robe off from him, and put his own raiment on him, and led him away to crucify him" (Matthew 27:31).

When they jerked the robe from Him, it must have been terrifically painful as the material ripped free from the dried blood that had coagulated on His open lacerations. It is hard to imagine the level of intense agony Jesus must have felt from head to toe, and the fact that He was still able to mentally and physically function after all that torture is a miracle in itself.

One Day Every Knee Will Bow Before Jesus Christ!

Although it may seem as though these Roman soldiers — who mocked Jesus and hailed Him as a king in contempt and ridicule — got away with their abominable actions, it was only temporary. One day in the near future, they will stand before the Mighty One whom they mocked and horrifically abused to give an account for their actions.

When that day comes, bowing before Jesus will be no laughing matter. In that future moment, everyone — including those very soldiers who mocked Jesus — will bow to their knees and proclaim that Jesus Christ is Lord!

In fact, a day is soon approaching when the entire human race will bow their knees to declare that Jesus is the King of kings and Lord of lords. Philippians 2:10 and 11 declares:

> **That at the name of Jesus every knee should bow, of things in heaven, and things in earth, and things under the earth; and that every tongue should confess that Jesus Christ is Lord, to the glory of God the Father.**

Friend, the Roman scourging and the additional torture of the Roman soldiers were what Jesus experienced *before* His crucifixion. In our next lesson, we will take a close look at what being crucified involved and Jesus final hours of suffering on a hill called Golgotha.

STUDY QUESTIONS

Study to shew thyself approved unto God, a workman that needeth not to be ashamed, rightly dividing the word of truth.
— 2 Timothy 2:15

1. When you think about God's promise of healing, what scriptures come to mind? Along with Isaiah 53:5 and First Peter 2:24, consider Exodus 15:26; Deuteronomy 7:15; Psalm 103:1-3; Proverbs 4:20-22; Mark 16:17 and 18; James 5:14-16; and Third John 2. How do these passages encourage you to truly believe God wants to heal you?

2. In addition to taking away our sickness, Jesus also took upon Himself all our *shame, guilt*, and *condemnation*. The enemy often brings these three "mega" feelings against us to overwhelm us and shut us down. But IN CHRIST, you are FREE from all three! To renew your mind and gain the upper hand over these feelings, look up, write down, and commit to memory these verses:

   • You are *not condemned* – John 3:17,18; Romans 8:1,2,33,34; 1 John 3:20

   • You have *no shame or guilt* – Isaiah 50:7-9; Romans 9:33; Philippians 1:20; Hebrews 9:11-14

   • *God loves you* and nothing can change that – Romans 8:31-39

PRACTICAL APPLICATION

But be ye doers of the word, and not hearers only, deceiving your own selves.
— James 1:22

1. Along with the torturous crucifixion, Jesus was also *scourged*. Before reading this lesson, what was your understanding of this Roman thrashing that Christ received? Of all the new insights you have learned, what touched you most deeply? Why?

2. How does this fresh perspective of the Roman scourge that Jesus endured impact your love and appreciation for Him?

3. First Peter 2:24 and Isaiah 53:5 both declare that by Jesus' stripes, you are healed. He paid an indescribably high price to purchase your physical healing. Have you been tolerating sickness somewhere in your body? If so, where? Pause and pray, "Father, give me Your grace to begin standing on and speaking Your promises of healing out loud over my life and against the enemy, until it becomes a reality in me. In Jesus' name, amen!"

---

1 "Church History (Book IV), Chapter 15. Under Verus, Polycarp with Others suffered Martyrdom at Smyrna." Translated by Arthur Cushman McGiffert, NewAdvent.org, https://www.newadvent.org/fathers/250104.htm. Accessed October 17, 2024.

TOPIC

Golgotha — 'The Place of the Skull'

SCRIPTURES

1. **Luke 23:38** — And a superscription also was written over him in letters of Greek, and Latin, and Hebrew, This Is The King Of The Jews.

2. **Matthew 27:32** — And as they came out, they found a man of Cyrene, Simon by name: him they compelled to bear his cross.

3. **Matthew 27:33** — And when they were come unto a place called Golgotha, that is to say, a place of a skull.

4. **Matthew 27:51** — And, behold, the veil of the temple was rent in twain from the top to the bottom; and the earth did quake, and the rocks rent.

5. **1 Corinthians 15:3,4** — …Christ died for our sins according to the scriptures; and that he was buried, and that he rose again the third day according to the scriptures.

6. **Matthew 27:34** — They gave him vinegar to drink mingled with gall.…

7. **Matthew 27:35** — And they crucified him.…

8. **Deuteronomy 21:22,23** — And if a man have committed a sin worthy of death, and he be to be put to death, and thou hang him on a tree: his body shall not remain all night upon the tree, but thou shalt in any wise bury him that day; (for he that is hanged is accursed of God)....

9. **John 19:28** — ...Jesus...saith, I thirst.

10. **John 19:33,34** — But when they came to Jesus, and saw that he was dead already, they brake not his legs: but one of the soldiers with a spear pierced his side, and forthwith came there out blood and water.

11. **Matthew 27:36** — And sitting down they watched him there.

12. **1 Peter 1:18,19** — Forasmuch as ye know that ye were not redeemed with corruptible things, as silver and gold, from your vain conversation received by tradition from your fathers; but with the precious blood of Christ, as of a lamb without blemish and without spot.

13. **Isaiah 53:3-5** — He is despised and rejected of men; a man of sorrows, and acquainted with grief: and we hid as it were our faces from him; he was despised, and we esteemed him not. Surely he hath borne our griefs, and carried our sorrows: yet we did esteem him stricken, smitten of God, and afflicted. But he was wounded for our transgressions, he was bruised for our iniquities: the chastisement of our peace was upon him; and with his stripes we are healed.

GREEK WORDS

1. "compelled" — to compel, to coerce, to constrain, or to force someone into some kind of compulsory service

2. "gall" (*chole*) — refers to a special painkiller

3. "crucified" — an upright, pointed stake that was used to punish of criminals; used to describe those who were hung up, impaled, or beheaded and then publicly displayed; also used in connection with public execution; the point of hanging a criminal publicly was to bring further humiliation to the accused

SYNOPSIS

Jesus Christ was crucified more than 2,000 years ago on a hill called Golgotha. The Roman emperor Hadrian, who hated everything about Jesus and Christianity, is said to have built a pagan temple on top of Jesus' tomb in the Second Century, to hide it from public view. But when Emperor Constantine converted to Christianity in about 312 AD, that pagan temple was demolished, and a church was built in its place to commemorate the site where Jesus gave His life for our redemption. Today, the Church of the Holy Sepulchre continues to welcome visitors from around the world and offers tangible proof of Christ's victory over the grave.

The emphasis of this lesson:

Crucifixion was a ghastly, torturous death reserved for criminals. Jesus died this kind of death for us. He was nailed to the Cross and bore the sin of humanity in Himself. He gave His life's blood to redeem us. And because of His sacrifice, we will spend eternity with Him!

Two Sites Claim To Be Golgotha

Today in the city of Jerusalem, there are two different alleged sites of Jesus's crucifixion called "Golgotha." One of these is called the Garden Tomb or Gordon's Tomb, and the reason it is often referred to as Gordon's Tomb is because Major-General Charles Gordon from England visited this site in 1883. Gordon believed it to be Jesus' tomb because a cliff nearby had a natural formation that seemed to display the face of a skull carved into the rocks. Although the image of a skull is only barely perceptible today, nevertheless, it became known as Gordon's Tomb.

Today, while this site is managed by the Garden Tomb Association, they do not state that the Garden Tomb was Jesus' actual tomb from which He resurrected, but that it was similar to the garden tomb where Jesus was placed after His crucifixion. Many Christians prefer the Garden Tomb, and we will see why in a moment.

The other possible site for Jesus' tomb is found inside the Church of the Holy Sepulchre. This site is covered with a great deal of religious decorations, which repels Protestant Christians. However, it is most likely the real Golgotha and tomb of Jesus, because history is on the side of the Church of the Holy Sepulchre.

When Emperor Constantine came to faith and declared the Roman Empire to be Christian, his mother, Helena, was very committed to her faith in Christ. Accordingly, she came to Israel and began searching for holy sites associated with the life of Jesus. After interviewing several people, Helena found the location where Jesus was crucified, Golgotha, along with the tomb from which He was resurrected. Eventually, a church was built over the site.

Again, because the Church of the Holy Sepulchre is covered with a large amount of religious ornamentation, most Christians prefer the Garden Tomb or Gordon's Tomb because of its simplicity and natural, untouched appearance. But the Church of the Holy Sepulchre does seem to be the historical site of Jesus' crucifixion, burial, and resurrection.

Why Is Golgotha So Small?

Often, those who visit Jerusalem ask, "Where is the mountain of Golgotha?" And the answer is that it is right inside the Church of the Holy Sepulchre. There you can ascend a set of steps to the top of what remains of Golgotha. Of course, when most people see it, they ask, "Is this all there is? Where is the rest of it?"

In 1172, Italian architects began to construct the Tower of Pisa in Italy, and the same architects also constructed a cathedral nearby called the Cathedral of Pisa. Wealthy religious families in the area wanted to be buried in holy ground. In their minds, there was no holier ground than Golgotha, so they dispatched workers to Jerusalem to chip away at the real Golgotha where Jesus was crucified.

During the 12th Century, the soil of Golgotha was loaded into five ships that transported the sacred soil from the Holy Land to the Cathedral Square in Pisa, Italy where it was used in a cemetery — Campo Santo or Camposanto Monumentale — so that wealthy religious families could be buried in the sacred soil of Golgotha.

That is why when visitors come to see the traditional site of Golgotha inside the Church of the Holy Sepulchre, it often fails to meet their imagination of what Golgotha looked like when Jesus was crucified 2,000 years ago. If you want to see the remainder of Golgotha, you must travel to Pisa, Italy, where that sacred soil was used in the cemetery at the Cathedral of Pisa.

Jesus Carried His Own 'Cross'

After Jesus was scourged, He carried the upper portion of His Cross — the crossbeam — all the way to a hill that was called Golgotha, which can be seen today inside the Church of the Holy Sepulchre.

When most people think of a cross, they visually think of what looks like a plus sign that typically adorns churches or jewelry. However, Romans in the First Century did not use crosses shaped like that. Traditional crosses are an image created by painters during the Middle Ages that eventually carried over into modern times.

In reality, Roman crosses during Jesus' day were shaped like a "T." They were made of a tall, upright post, that had a notched groove at the top, into which a crossbeam was placed after a victim had been tied or nailed to it. The crossbeam normally weighed about 100 pounds, and it was carried on the back of the victim to the place of execution.

Because Roman law dictated that a criminal was to carry his own cross to the place of execution, Jesus was forced to carry His extremely heavy crossbeam on His back all the way to Golgotha. You can imagine how difficult this was, knowing that He had already been scourged and horrifically abused. His back and body had literally been ripped open and was flowing with blood, and now a hundred-pound crossbeam was placed across His shoulders.

The purpose of victims being made to carry their own cross was so bystanders who were watching were reminded of Rome's power and the need of each subject to comply with Roman authority lest they suffer a similar fate.

A Sign for All To See

What you may not know is that as the crossbeam was laid across the victim's back, a person often walked ahead of him to proclaim his crime to those who were standing by the sides of the road watching as the criminal carried the crossbeam to the place of execution.

There was also a sign hung around the neck of the person carrying the crossbeam, and like the herald, the purpose of the sign was to give the person's name and announce his crime and the reason for which he was being crucified. The sign could easily be read by bystanders lining the streets, and it was normally written in Hebrew, Greek, and Latin. This sign was later hung on the cross above the victim's head.

In Jesus' case, "…a superscription also was written over him in letters of Greek, and Latin, and Hebrew, THIS IS THE KING OF THE JEWS"

(Luke 23:38). The sign announced Jesus' crime — that He was King of the Jews — and was written in Hebrew, Greek, and Latin.

As Jesus walked to His crucifixion, this sign dangled from his neck and was ultimately hung above His head on the Cross so that all who saw Him knew exactly what charge had been leveled against Him (*see* John 19:19,20).

Jesus Was Assisted by Simon of Cyrene

Carrying a hundred-pound crossbeam for such a long distance would be difficult for any man — but it was especially burdensome for Jesus who had been beaten so severely and was so weak. According to John's gospel, it seems Jesus began His journey to Calvary carrying His own Cross, but at some point, He quickly became unable to continue.

It was then that the Roman soldiers forced Simon of Cyrene to help because Jesus was so exhausted from what He had already suffered. Matthew informs us:

And as they came out, they found a man of Cyrene, Simon by name: him they compelled to bear his cross.
— Matthew 27:32

In this passage, the word "compelled" in Greek means *to compel, to coerce, to constrain*, or *to force someone into some kind of compulsory service*. All three synoptic gospels mention this man Simon who was forced to carry Jesus' Cross. Mark said he was the father of Alexander and Rufus, and he was coming from the country at the time.

Eventually, Jesus arrived at the place of execution — Golgotha in Hebrew and Aramaic, Calvary in Latin. This is confirmed in Matthew 27:33, which says, "…They were come unto a place called Golgotha, that is to say, a place of a skull."

There, vultures could be seen flying overhead as they waited to devour the dying carcasses left hanging on crosses. In the nearby wilderness, wild dogs anxiously waited for the newest dead bodies that would eventually be dumped by executioners, and that would become the dog's next meal. Everything about a crucifixion site was disgusting and wretched.

Writings by Early Church Leaders About Golgotha

When you study what early Church Fathers wrote about Golgotha, you will discover that there is a different reason as to why the site was named "The Place of the Skull." For example, Origen — who was noted as one of the most important early Church Fathers and known for his accuracy — wrote that Jesus was crucified on the spot where Adam was buried.

Whether or not this is true, there really was an early widespread Christian belief that Jesus was crucified above the place where Adam was buried. Matthew 27:51 says that an earthquake occurred while Jesus hung on the cross, and early tradition says during that quake, His blood ran down the Cross, into a crack in the rock below, and it drained through that crevice until it fell on the skull of Adam.

This belief was so entrenched in early Christian tradition that Jerome — who was one of the most prominent scholars of the Early Church that translated the Bible from Hebrew and Greek into Latin — referred to this in a letter that he wrote in 386 AD. He affirmed that Jesus really was crucified on the place where Adam was buried and that the blood of Jesus dripped down, ran through a crevice, and fell upon the skull of Adam.

Although this is unknown to most Western believers, it is so accepted in early Christian history that it is a major theme of Orthodox doctrine. In fact, it is the reason why the skull of Adam appears consistently at the base of the Cross in both Orthodox paintings and icons. Most people assume that it symbolizes Jesus' victory over death but, in fact, it symbolizes Adam's skull.

If you ever see a skull at the base of a crucifix, now you will know that it symbolizes Adam's skull that was allegedly found buried at the site of Jesus' crucifixion. If this is true, it is amazing that the Second Adam — Jesus Christ — died for the sins of the world exactly on the spot where the first Adam, the original sinner, was buried.

Likewise, if Jesus' blood ran down the crack in the stone and fell upon Adam's skull, as this early tradition says, it would be very symbolic of Jesus' blood washing away all the sin of the human race that originated with Adam's disobedience.

Jesus Knew He Was To Drink the Full Cup of Suffering

Jesus was crucified like a criminal just outside the walls of Jerusalem. Rather than arguing about which location is correct, we should be rejoicing in the truth that Jesus was crucified for our salvation! The apostle Paul declared:

> **...Christ died for our sins according to the scriptures; and that he was buried, and that he rose again the third day according to the scriptures.**
>
> **— 1 Corinthians 15:3,4**

What is important is not where the event took place, but that it *did* take place. Jesus was indeed crucified, and He shed His blood to purchase the forgiveness of mankind's sin and restore our relationship with the Father!

God's Word also says:

> **They gave him vinegar to drink mingled with gall: and when he had tasted thereof, he would not drink.**
>
> **— Matthew 27:34**

The word "gall" in Greek refers to *a special painkiller*. History tells us there was a group of kind women in the city of Jerusalem who believed it was their job to help anesthetize the pain of people who were dying horrific deaths. These women wanted to eliminate as much pain and misery as possible for the scores of people being crucified by the Romans.

Hence, they created a homemade brew of painkiller, and that is what was given to Jesus. Scripture notes this "gall" was offered to Jesus twice — once *before* His crucifixion and once while He was dying on the Cross (*see* Matthew 27:34,48). But He rejected it both times because He knew He was to drink the full cup of suffering.

Soldiers Cast Lots and Watched Jesus

Matthew 27:35 says, "And they crucified him, and parted his garments, casting lots: that it might be fulfilled which was spoken by the prophet, They parted my garments among them, and upon my vesture did they cast lots."

Jewish law required that the person being crucified was to be stripped naked. Thus, when Jesus was crucified, He hung naked on the Cross. This was part of the humiliation Christ suffered on our behalf. And according to Roman custom, the soldiers who carried out the crucifixion had a right to the victim's clothes.

The gospel of John says, "Then the soldiers, when they had crucified Jesus, took his garments, and made four parts, to every soldier a part; and also his coat: now the coat was without seam, woven from the top throughout. They said therefore among themselves, Let us not rend it, but cast lots for it..." (John 19:23,24).

The "four parts" of clothing distributed among them were Jesus' head gear, sandals, girdle, and the tallith, or the outer garment that had fringes on the bottom. This outer garment, or "coat" — which was "without seam" — was specially handmade and therefore an expensive piece of clothing.

Normally, the coat itself would have also been divided among them, but because the garment was so valuable, the soldiers chose to cast lots for the whole thing instead. The words "casting lots" referred to a game of chance used to determine a winner.

As Jesus paid the price for redemption, the soldiers at the foot of the Cross played a game to see who would get His finest piece of clothing! After the soldiers finished casting lots, "sitting down they watched him there" (Matthew 27:36). The word "watched" is the Greek word *tereo*, which means *to guard*. The Greek tense here means *to consistently guard* or *to consistently be on the watch*. It was the responsibility of these soldiers to maintain order at the crucifixion site. Specifically, they were on duty to ensure no one came to rescue Jesus and that He remained crucified until they could confirm His death.

In Greek, the word "crucified" (*see* Matthew 27:35; Mark 15:24,25; Luke 23:33; John 19:17,18) refers to *an upright, pointed stake that was used to punish criminals*. This term was used to describe *those who were hung up, impaled, or beheaded and then publicly displayed*. Thus, it was a word used in connection with public execution. A crucifixion was a gruesome event, and the point of publicly punishing a criminal in this way was to bring further humiliation to the accused, which is exactly what happened to Jesus.

The Roman Crucifixion

Different parts of the world practiced different kinds of crucifixion. For example, in the East, the victim was beheaded then publicly displayed. But among the Jews, the victim was usually stoned and then hung on a tree. That is why we read in Deuteronomy 21:22 and 23:

And if a man have committed a sin worthy of death, and he be to be put to death, and thou hang him on a tree: his body shall not remain all night upon the tree, but thou shalt in any wise bury him that day; (for he that is hanged is accursed of God)....

Clearly, crucifixion was one of the cruelest and most barbaric forms of punishment in the ancient world. In fact, it was so horrible that noted historian Flavius Josephus wrote that it was "the most wretched of deaths," and it was viewed with such horror that in one of Seneca's letters to Lucilius, Seneca stated that suicide was preferable to crucifixion. At the time Jesus was crucified, crucifixion was entirely in the hands of the *Romans*. What follows is a brief overview of a Roman crucifixion.

1. THE CROSSBEAM AND THE NAILS

Once the accused reached the place of crucifixion, he was laid on the crossbeam he carried. Soldiers would then stretch the victim's arms out (which is what they did to Jesus) and then drive a five-inch nail through each of his wrists — not the palms of his hands — into the crossbeam.

After being nailed to the crossbeam, the victim was hoisted up by a rope, and the crossbeam was dropped into a notch on top of the upright post. When the crossbeam dropped into the groove, the victim suffered excruciating pain as his hands and wrists were wrenched by the sudden jerking motion. Eventually, the weight of the victim's body caused his arms to be pulled out of their sockets.

Once the victim's wrists were secured in place on the crossbeam, the feet came next. Usually, the feet were nailed through the ankles into the sides of the upright beam. A long nail was driven between the ankle bones to prevent it from tearing as the victim arched upward, gasping for breath.

Josephus wrote about the Roman soldiers: that the Roman soldiers "out of rage and hatred amused themselves by nailing their prisoners in different postures."[1]

2. The Process of Asphyxiation

For the victim to breathe, he had to push himself up by his feet, which were nailed to the vertical beam. But because the pressure on his ankles became unbearable, it wasn't possible for him to remain long in that position, so eventually he would collapse back into the hanging position.

As the victim pushed up and collapsed back down again and again over a long period of time, his shoulders eventually dislocated and popped out of joint. Soon the out-of-joint shoulders were followed by the elbows and wrists. These various dislocations caused the arms to be extended up to nine inches longer than usual, resulting in terrible cramps in the victim's arm muscles and making it impossible for him to push himself upward to breathe any longer.

Jesus experienced all this torture, and when He was finally too exhausted and could no longer push Himself upward on the nail lodged in His feet, the process of asphyxiation began. When He dropped down with the full weight of His body on the nails that were driven through His wrists, it sent horrific, excruciating pain up His arms to register in His brain.

Added to this torture was the agony caused by the constant grating of Jesus' recently scourged back against the upright post every time He pushed up to breathe and then collapsed back to a hanging position. Then, due to extreme loss of blood and hyperventilation, the victim would begin to experience severe dehydration. We can see this process in Jesus' own crucifixion when He cried out, "…I thirst" (John 19:28).

After several hours of this torment, the victim's heart would begin to fail. Next his lungs would collapse, and excess fluids would begin filling the lining of his heart and lungs, adding to the slow process of asphyxiation. A person that was crucified eventually drowned in his own fluids, which filled his lungs.

3. The Purpose of Breaking the Victim's Legs

The Scripture says, "But when they came to Jesus, and saw that he was dead already, they brake not his legs: but one of the soldiers with a spear pierced his side, and forthwith came there out blood and water" (John 19:33,34).

When the Roman soldier came to determine whether Jesus was alive, he thrust his spear into Jesus' side. The Bible tells us that blood and water came pouring forth from the wound the spear had made in Jesus' side, which was evidence that Jesus' heart and lungs had shut down and were now filled with fluid. This was enough to assure the soldier that Jesus was already dead.

It was customary for Roman soldiers to break the lower leg bones of a person being crucified, making it impossible for the victim to push himself upward to breathe and thus causing him to asphyxiate at a much quicker rate. However, because blood and water gushed from Jesus' side, the soldier knew He was already dead. Thus, there was no reason for Jesus' legs to be broken. This is a *brief taste* of a Roman crucifixion.

We Need To Remember What the Cross Was Really Like!

Today, the Cross has become a fashion item that is decorated with gems, rhinestones, gold, and silver. Crosses adorn women's ears and dangle at the bottom of gold chains and necklaces. The cross tops steeples on churches and is an adornment in altars inside churches. The symbol of the cross is even tattooed on people's flesh.

Although there is nothing wrong with adorning ourselves with the Cross, in beautifying the Cross to make it pleasing to look upon, many have forgotten the utter humiliation and the true picture of what Christ endured as He hung there and died a slow, torturous death.

The Cross was shocking and appalling. It was a disgusting, repulsive, nauseating, stomach-turning sight. Blood drenched Jesus' torso, it poured from His head and brow, and it ran like rivers from the deeply torn flesh in His hands and feet. Even Jesus' eyes were matted with the blood from the wounds in His brow. His head bled from the crown of thorns the soldiers pushed on His head.

Thus, the whole scene was ugly, unsightly, repulsive, sickening, vile, foul, and revolting. The apostle Peter knew what the crucifixion entailed and all the bloodshed that took place as Jesus gave His very life for us. Here is what he wrote under the inspiration of the Holy Spirit for us to remember:

> **Forasmuch as ye know that ye were not redeemed with corruptible things, as silver and gold, from your vain conversation**

**received by tradition from your fathers; but with the precious
blood of Christ, as of a lamb without blemish and without spot.**
— 1 Peter 1:18,19

Friends, we need to understand and appreciate the price Jesus paid for our redemption. As believers, it is good for us to take time to reflect on what the Cross of Jesus Christ was really like. When we fail to remember what it cost Him to save us and heal us, we begin to lose our gratitude for Him and even treat our salvation with contempt. It is only when we purposely choose to remember all that Jesus went through that we can begin to sincerely appreciate the unbelievable price He paid for our redemption.

In the next lesson, we will learn why Jesus cried out "IT IS FINISHED!"

STUDY QUESTIONS

**Study to shew thyself approved unto God, a workman that
needeth not to be ashamed, rightly dividing the word of truth.**
— 2 Timothy 2:15

1. In this lesson, there were many details presented about the actual location of Jesus' death, the historical description of First-Century crosses, the meaning of the word "gall," and what early Church Fathers believed and taught about Golgotha. What new facts fascinated you most? And what did you learn about the crucifixion that you didn't previously know?

2. One of the names for Jesus in Scripture is the *last Adam*, who came to *undo* all the first Adam did through his disobedience. Carefully read Romans 5:12-19 and First Corinthians 15:21, 22, and 45-49 and note the stark differences between the first Adam and the last Adam, Jesus Christ.

3. As Jesus experienced the Roman scourging, the crown of thorns, the nails in His wrists and feet, and the spear in His side, a tremendous amount of His blood was shed. Friend, the blood of Jesus is priceless! Take some time to reflect on these verses and share what the blood of Christ means to *you* personally.

    - His blood provides forgiveness – Matthew 26:28

    - His blood purchased us – Acts 20:28; 1 Peter 1:18 and 19

    - His blood justified us – Romans 5:9; Revelation 1:5

- His blood cleansed and purified us – Hebrews 9:11-14; 1 John 1:7
- His blood provided peace – Colossians 1:20-22
- His blood opened the door to the Father's presence – Hebrews 10:19-22

PRACTICAL APPLICATION

**But be ye doers of the word, and not hearers only,
deceiving your own selves.
—James 1:22**

1. What are the benefits of taking time to remember the scourge, the Cross, and the abuse Jesus endured at the hands of the religious leaders and Romans?

2. When Jesus was crucified, a sign was nailed above His head declaring His crime (*see* Luke 23:38). The truth is, *we* were the sinners who deserved to die, not Jesus. What does Colossians 2:13-15 say symbolically happened to the "sign" declaring your crimes when Jesus died in your place?

3. Take a moment to think about all the things for which Jesus has forgiven you. Those are the things that would have been written above your head for all the world to see had Jesus not paid the penalty for your sins. Why not take a moment to thank Him and Praise Him for His matchless mercy and forgiveness! You are truly blessed! (*See* Psalm 32:1,2.)

---

[1] Of the War – Book V, CHAPTER 11, www.penelope.uchicago.edu, https://penelope.uchicago.edu/josephus/war-5.html. Accessed October 18, 2024.

TOPIC

'IT IS FINISHED!'

SCRIPTURES

1. **John 19:30** — When Jesus therefore had received the vinegar, he said, It is finished: and he bowed his head, and gave up the ghost.
2. **Matthew 27:51** — And, behold, the veil of the temple was rent in twain from the top to the bottom; and the earth did quake, and the rocks rent.
3. **Hebrews 9:12** — Neither by the blood of goats and calves, but by his own blood he entered in once into the holy place, having obtained eternal redemption for us.
4. **Colossians 1:14** — In whom we have redemption through his blood, even the forgiveness of sins.
5. **Isaiah 53:4,5** — Surely he hath borne our griefs, and carried our sorrows: yet we did esteem him stricken, smitten of God, and afflicted. But he was wounded for our transgressions, he was bruised for our iniquities: the chastisement of our peace was upon him; and with his stripes we are healed.
6. **Matthew 27:50** — Jesus, when he had cried again with a loud voice, yielded up the ghost.
7. **Ephesians 2:14** — For he is our peace, who hath made both one, and hath broken down the middle wall of partition between us.
8. **Matthew 27:51** — ...The earth did quake, and the rocks rent.
9. **Hebrews 10:19** — Having therefore, brethren, boldness to enter into the holiest by the blood of Jesus.

GREEK WORDS

1. "behold" (*idou*) — amazement, shock, and wonder
2. "It is finished" — (*Tetelestai*): to end; to bring to completion; to bring to a conclusion; to complete; to accomplish; to fulfill; or to finish; one scholar notes that anything that has reached this state has arrived at completion, maturity, or perfection

3. "earth" (*ges*) — the whole earth
4. "quake" (*seiso*) — to shake; to agitate; to create a commotion; where we get the word for a seismograph, the apparatus that registers the intensity of an earthquake
5. "rocks" (*petra*) — large rocks; huge rocks
6. "rent" (*schidzo*) — to rend, to tear, to violently tear asunder, or to terribly fracture

SYNOPSIS

The apostle John was the only known apostle to be present at Jesus' crucifixion, and in his gospel, he recorded the Lord's very last words. He said, "When Jesus therefore had received the vinegar, he said, *It is finished*: and he bowed his head, and gave up the ghost" (John 19:30). In this lesson, we will learn the deeper meaning of these three words and why the veil in the Jewish temple split from top to bottom the moment Jesus died.

The emphasis of this lesson:

Jesus' final words on the Cross were "It is finished!" In that defining moment, the veil in the Temple ripped in two, and Jesus conveyed four important messages to the Father and to the world: (1) the mission is accomplished; (2) the sacrifice is complete and finished; (3) all debt is paid in full; and (4) the old has ended, the new has begun.

Jesus' Last Words Released a Supernatural Shockwave

The gospels of John and Matthew give us insight into the very moment Jesus died on the Cross. As we saw in the introduction, John was there when Jesus said, "It is finished" and when He bowed his head and "gave up the ghost" (John 19:30). And in Matthew 27:51, it says that when Jesus died, "…Behold, the veil of the temple was rent in twain from the top to the bottom; and the earth did quake, and the rocks rent."

Notice the word "behold" in Matthew 27:51. It is the Greek word *idou*, and it pictures *amazement*, *shock*, and *wonder*. It is the equivalent of Matthew getting very excited as he relates what took place. Thus, we could translate this verse, "Wow! Listen to this! It is shocking! When Jesus said, 'It is finished,' and He died on the Cross, amazingly, the veil in the Temple was rent in twain from top to bottom; and the earth did quake, and the rocks rent!"

There were two veils inside the Temple — one at the entrance to the Holy Place and a second at the entrance to the Holy of Holies. Only the high priest was allowed to pass through the second veil once a year during the Festival of Atonement, and that second veil was massive and represented a barrier between the sinfulness of man and the presence of God inside the Holy of Holies.

The Veil to the Holy of Holies

In his book *The Life and Times of Jesus the Messiah*, Alfred Edersheim wrote about the size and weight of the second veil at the entrance to the Holy of Holies and also talked about the manpower needed to manipulate or move it due to its enormous size. Edersheim said:

> **The Veils before the Most Holy Place were 40 cubits (60 feet) long, and 20 (30 feet) wide, of the thickness of the palm of the hand, and wrought in 72 squares, which were joined together; and these Veils were so heavy, that, in the exaggerated language of the time, it needed 3000 [300] priests to manipulate each. If the Veil was at all such as is described in the Talmud, it could not have been rent in twain by a mere earthquake or the fall of the lintel, although its composition in squares fastened together might explain, how the rent might be as described in the Gospel.**[1]

So you can gather from Edersheim's description that this second veil was absolutely massive.

Scholar Maurice Henry Harris wrote of the enormity and weight of the veil, telling us:

> **Three hundred priests were told off [or they were designated] to draw the veil (of the Temple) aside…the thickness of the veil was a handbreadth. It was woven of seventy-two cords, and each cord consisted of twenty-four strands. It was forty cubits long and twenty wide…. When it became soiled, it took three hundred priests to immerse and cleanse it.**[2]

At the very moment that Jesus was breathing His last breath on the cross at Golgotha, the high priest was standing at his station in the Temple. In the instant Jesus exclaimed, "It is finished!" — deep inside the Temple — an inexplicable, mystifying supernatural event occurred.

The massive, fortified veil that stood before the Holy of Holies was suddenly split in half from the top all the way to the bottom! The sound of that veil splitting must have been deafening as it ripped and tore, starting from the top and going all the way down to the floor. It was as if invisible, divine hands had reached out to grab it, rip it to shreds, and discard it.

Imagine how shocked the high priest must have been when he heard the ripping sounds inside the Temple and then watched as the veil was torn in half, leaving the two sides of the once-massive curtain lying collapsed to his right and his left.

What God declared through this supernatural event is that when Jesus was lifted up on the Cross and He sacrificed His sinless life, it was no longer necessary for a high priest to continually make sacrifices year after year — because Jesus' blood settled man's sin issue forever!

That is why God Himself reached out with invisible hands and took hold of the veil of the Temple and ripped it in half. He was declaring that the way to the Holy of Holies was now available to everyone who came to Him through the blood of Jesus!

FOUR MEANINGS TO JESUS' WORDS 'IT IS FINISHED!'

Turning our attention once more to John 19:30, we read, "When Jesus therefore had received the vinegar, he said, *It is finished*: and he bowed his head, and gave up the ghost."

Those three words — "It is finished" — are a translation of the Greek word *Tetelestai*, which means *to end*; *to bring to completion*; *to bring to a conclusion*; *to complete*; *to accomplish*; *to fulfill*; or *to finish*. One scholar notes that anything that has reached this state has arrived at completion, maturity, or perfection.

What is interesting about this word *Tetelestai* is that there were many nuances to it. For the remainder of this lesson, we are going to focus on four primary meanings conveyed in these words that have significance to Christ's sacrifice.

MEANING ONE: THE MISSION IS ACCOMPLISHED!

First, the word *Tetelestai* was Jesus' exclamation that *He had finished the work the Father had sent Him to do.* One writer has noted that when a servant was sent on a mission and then later returned to his master, the servant would say, "*Tetelestai*" — meaning, *"I have done exactly what you requested"* or *"The mission is now accomplished."* When Jesus said, "*Tetelestai* — It is finished," He was exclaiming to the entire universe that He had faithfully fulfilled the Father's will, and the mission was now accomplished.

No wonder Jesus shouted those words. This was the greatest victory in the history of the human race! He had been faithful to His assignment, even in the face of unfathomable challenges. Now the fight was over, and Jesus could cry out to the Father, "*Tetelestai* — *I have done exactly what You asked Me to do!"* or *"The mission is accomplished!"*

MEANING TWO: THE SACRIFICE IS COMPLETE AND FINISHED

Second, the word *Tetelestai* was the equivalent of the Hebrew word spoken by the high priest when he presented a sacrificial lamb without spot or blemish. Annually the high priest entered the Holy of Holies, where he poured the blood of that sacrificial spotless lamb on the mercy seat of the Ark of the Covenant. The moment that blood touched the mercy seat, atonement was made for the people's sins for one more year — when once again, the high priest would enter beyond the veil of that sacred room to offer blood. This was done annually to obtain temporary forgiveness of sin.

But when Jesus hung on the Cross, He was both Lamb and High Priest. In that holy moment, as our Great High Priest, Jesus offered His own blood for the permanent removal of sin. He offered up the perfect sacrifice — and in that instant, there remained no more need for additional offerings for sin.

Hebrews 9:12 declares, "Neither by the blood of goats and calves, but by his [Jesus'] own blood he entered in once into the holy place, having obtained eternal redemption for us."

So when Jesus said, "It is finished — *Tetelestai*," He was declaring the end of sacrifice, because the ultimate Sacrifice had been made! Atonement was completed, perfected, and fully accomplished. It was done once and for all — finished forever!

Meaning Three: All Debt Is Paid in Full

Third, the word *Tetelestai* was used in the business world to signify *the full payment of a debt*. When a debt had been fully paid off, the parchment on which the debt was recorded was stamped with the words *Tetelestai*, which meant *the debt had been paid in full*.

This means that once a person calls Jesus the Lord of his life and personally accepts His sacrifice, no debt of sin exists for that person any longer. Our debt is wiped out because Jesus paid the price no sinner could ever pay.

When Jesus took our place, He paid the debt of sin we owed, and when we by faith repent and receive Him as Lord, we are set free! This is why Paul so gloriously wrote, "…We have redemption through his blood, even the forgiveness of sins" (Colossians 1:14).

When Jesus uttered those words, "It is finished," it was His divine declaration that the debt was fully satisfied, fulfilled, and complete. His blood utterly and completely cleansed us forever. His finished work was far-reaching and all-embracing for all of us who put our faith in Him.

Meaning Four: The Old Has Ended, the New Has Begun

Fourth, the word *Tetelestai* depicted *a turning point when one period ended, and another new period began*.

When Jesus exclaimed, "It is finished," it was indeed a turning point in the entire history of mankind, for at that moment the Old Testament came to an end — finished and closed — and the New Testament began.

The Cross is "the Great Divide" in human history. When Jesus cried out, "It is finished," He was essentially shouting, "The Old Covenant has ended, and the New Covenant has begun!"

Furthermore, when Jesus cried, "It is finished," He was declaring that every Old Testament prophecy about His earthly ministry and His dying for our sins was fulfilled. At that moment, the sacrifices of the Old Testament permanently ceased, for the perfect Sacrifice had laid down His life for the salvation of mankind.

Jesus' mission was accomplished, and He could cry out that His task was complete!

Isaiah Identifies
Six Blessings From Christ's Sacrifice

Because Jesus was willing to offer His own blood as the full payment of our sin debt, we are forgiven and utterly debt-free. "PAID IN FULL" has been stamped on our past sinful record because Jesus paid the price for our redemption with His own blood!

As a matter of fact, there are numerous blessings that we receive because of Christ's ultimate sacrifice. Isaiah said:

> **Surely he hath borne our griefs, and carried our sorrows: yet we did esteem him stricken, smitten of God, and afflicted. But he was wounded for our transgressions, he was bruised for our iniquities: the chastisement of our peace was upon him; and with his stripes we are healed.**
>
> **— Isaiah 53:4,5**

If you are consumed with grief, remember that *Jesus bore your grief.*

If you are overwhelmed with sorrows, remember that *Jesus carried your sorrows.*

If you are trapped in a life of transgression, remember that *Jesus was wounded for your transgressions.*

If you are living in sin, you can be forgiven because *Jesus was bruised for your iniquities.*

If you are tormented and have no peace, remember that *Jesus was chastised for your peace.*

And if you are physically or mentally sick, remember that *Jesus was wounded for your healing.*

THREE MAJOR EVENTS OCCURRED AT THE TIME OF JESUS' DEATH

The Sky Turned Dark

The Bible informs us of three supernatural happenings that took place when Jesus died. First, Matthew 27:45, Mark 15:33, and Luke 23:45 all document that when Jesus died, the sky darkened, and it started at the sixth hour, which would be at about noon — the time of day when the sun is at its brightest. Traditionally, the sixth hour was also the very moment when the high priest, who was arrayed in his full priestly garments, began the procession in which he would enter the Temple courts to slaughter a pure, spotless Passover lamb.

This darkness that covered the land lasted until the ninth hour — about the time when the sacrifices of the Passover lambs would be coming to an end. It was at this moment that Jesus cried out, "It is finished — *Tetelestai!*" All these elements were divinely synchronized by the hand of God.

THE TEMPLE VEIL WAS RIPPED IN TWO

The second event, which we mentioned earlier, involves the inner veil in the Temple. As Jesus breathed for the last time, He gathered just enough air to speak forth a victory shout. His assignment was complete! And according to Matthew 27:50, after proclaiming, "It is finished" with His last ounce of strength, "Jesus…yielded up the ghost."

It was at that very moment that God Himself ripped the veil of the Temple in half from top to bottom. It was His way of declaring that the way to the Holy of Holies was now available to everyone who came to Him through the blood of Jesus!

This is why the apostle Paul wrote, "For he [Jesus] is our peace, who hath made both one, and hath broken down the middle wall of partition between us" (Ephesians 2:14). The massive veil that hung inside the Temple in front of the Holy of Holies was ripped from the very top all the way to the very bottom.

THE EARTH TREMBLED

The third event that took place at the time of Jesus' death is also recorded in Matthew 27:51, which says, "…The earth did quake, and the rocks rent."

The Greek word for "earth" here signifies *the whole earth*, which means what took place was a worldwide event. And the Greek word for "quake" means *to shake*; *to agitate*; or *to create a commotion*. It is where we get the word for a *seismograph*, the apparatus that registers the intensity of an earthquake.

Origen, the early Christian leader who is esteemed for his accuracy, recorded that there were "great earthquakes" at the time of Jesus' crucifixion.

Isn't it interesting that while Israel rejected Jesus and the Roman authorities crucified Him, creation always recognized Him. Think about it. During His life on this earth:

- Waves and wind obeyed Him (Mark 4:37-41).
- Water turned to wine at His command (John 2:1-11).
- Fishes and bread multiplied at His touch (Matthew 14:15-21; 15:32-39).
- Water supported His weight as He crossed it (Matthew 14:25-27).
- The wind ceased when He spoke to it (Luke 8:22-25).

Likewise, the earth shook and trembled at the death of its Creator, for it instantly felt its loss. The earth shuddered so violently when Jesus died, even "…the rocks rent" (Matthew 27:51).

In the original Greek text, the word "rocks" describes *massive rocks* or *huge, large rocks*. And the word "rent" means *to rend, to tear, to violently tear asunder*, or *to terribly fracture*. Thus, the earthquake that occurred when Jesus died was serious!

These three events — the earthquake, the veil of the Temple being ripped in two, and the sky turning to darkness at the time of Jesus' death — were not coincidences. They were GOD-incidences!

Jesus Did His Part, and We Must Do Ours

Friend, the way to the Holy of Holies was opened for all who would believe and put their faith in the finished work of Jesus Christ. Hebrews 10:19 declares that we are to have "…boldness to enter into the holiest by the blood of Jesus."

Jesus has done His part — He has bought us with the price of His own blood (*see* 1 Corinthians 6:19,20; 1 Peter 1:18,19). The moment He was finished paying that price and cried out, "It is finished," the barrier that once stood between God and man was permanently removed as God reached out with His invisible hands and ripped the Temple veil in two.

Now it's up to us as believers to come boldly by faith into God's presence and receive the divine help He has already provided for us.

In our next lesson, we will examine the facts confirming that Jesus really did die on the Cross, He was buried in a tomb, and the tomb was sealed.

STUDY QUESTIONS

Study to shew thyself approved unto God, a workman that
needeth not to be ashamed, rightly dividing the word of truth.
— 2 Timothy 2:15

1. Take a moment to write down the four primary meanings of the words "It is finished" (*Tetelestai*). Of the four, which one is most meaningful to you? Why?

2. When you sincerely ask God to forgive you of sin, what does the Bible say He actually does? *See* Psalm 103:12; and Isaiah 43:25; 44:22; 55:7; Acts 3:19; Hebrews 8:12; 1 John 1:9.

3. Under the Old Testament system, a blood sacrifice had to be made every year to cover the sins of the people. Unlike Jesus' blood, the cleansing effect of animal's blood was *temporary*. To help you really grasp the power of Jesus' sacrifice, take some time to carefully read Hebrews 9:11-14 and 10:1-17, and write down what the Holy Spirit shows you about how the New Covenant through Jesus is far superior to the old one.

PRACTICAL APPLICATION

But be ye doers of the word, and not hearers only,
deceiving your own selves.
— James 1:22

1. When Jesus died, God Himself reached out with invisible hands and took hold of the veil of the Temple and ripped it in half. He was declaring that the way to the Holy of Holies is now available to everyone who comes to Him through the blood of Jesus! What does this amazing news speak to you? Are you taking advantage of this tremendous privilege? Are you entering God's presence regularly for all that you need?

2. As a believer, you have the privilege of coming into God's presence through the shed blood and broken body of Jesus (*see* Hebrews 10:19-22). And according to Ephesians 3:12 and Hebrews 4:16, you are to come *boldly* and *confidently* to receive whatever help you need. So what do you need? Is it peace of mind, financial provision, physical healing, or restoration of a relationship? Come to the Father, ask for what you need, and receive it by faith in Jesus' name! As you make your request, consider these

promises: Psalm 34:8-10; 84:11; John 14:13,14; 15:7,8; Romans 8:32; Second Corinthians 9:8.

TOPIC

Buried and Sealed

SCRIPTURES

1. **Mark 15:42,43** — And now when the even was come, because it was the preparation, that is, the day before the sabbath, Joseph of Arimathaea, an honourable counsellor, which also waited for the kingdom of God, came, and went in boldly unto Pilate, and craved the body of Jesus.

2. **Mark 15:44,45** — And Pilate marvelled if he were already dead: and calling unto him the centurion, he asked him whether he had been any while dead. And when he knew it of the centurion, he gave the body to Joseph.

3. **John 3:1** — There was a man of the Pharisees, named Nicodemus, a ruler of the Jews.

4. **John 19:39** — And there came also Nicodemus, which at the first came to Jesus by night, and brought a mixture of myrrh and aloes, about an hundred pound weight.

5. **John 19:40** — Then took they the body of Jesus, and wound it in linen clothes with the spices, as the manner of the Jews is to bury.

6. **Matthew 6:21** — For where your treasure is, there will your heart be also.

7. **John 19:41,42** — Now in the place where he was crucified there was a garden; and in the garden a new sepulchre, wherein was never man yet laid. There laid they Jesus therefore because of the Jews' preparation day; for the sepulchre was nigh at hand.

8. **Isaiah 53:9** — And he made his grave...with the rich in his death....

9. **Luke 23:55** — And the women also, which came with him from Galilee, followed after, and beheld the sepulchre, and how his body was laid.

10. **Mark 15:46,47** — And he bought fine linen, and took him down, and wrapped him in the linen, and laid him in a sepulchre which was hewn out of a rock, and rolled a stone unto the door of the sepulchre. And Mary Magdalene and Mary the mother of Joses beheld where he was laid.

11. **Matthew 27:60** — …And he [Joseph of Arimathea] rolled a great stone to the door of the sepulchre, and departed.

12. **Matthew 27:63,64** — Saying, Sir, we remember that that deceiver said, while he was yet alive, After three days I will rise again. Command therefore that the sepulchre be made sure until the third day, lest his disciples come by night, and steal him away, and say unto the people, He is risen from the dead: so the last error shall be worse than the first.

13. **Matthew 27:65** — Pilate said unto them, Ye have a watch: go your way, make it as sure as ye can.

14. **Matthew 27:66** — So they went, and made the sepulchre sure, sealing the stone, and setting a watch.

15. **Acts 2:24** — Whom God hath raised up, having loosed the pains of death: because it was not possible that he should be holden of it.

GREEK WORDS

1. "honorable" (*euschemon*) — people who have a good reputation; people who have a good standing in society; or people who are prominent, influential, and wealthy

2. "counselor" (*bouleutes*) — depicts a member of the Sanhedrin

3. "craved" (*aiteo*) — to be adamant in requesting and demanding something

4. "body" (*ptoma*) — a dead body; often translated as corpse

5. "ruler" (*archon*) — chief one, ruler, or prince; denoted the rulers of local synagogues and members of the Sanhedrin who were the highest authorities in the land

6. "myrrh" (*smurna*) — an expensive yellowish-brown, sweet-smelling gum resin that was obtained from a tree and had a bitter taste; chiefly used as a chemical for embalming the dead

7. "aloes" (*aloe*) — a sweet-smelling fragrance derived from the juice pressed from the leaves of a tree found in the Middle East; used to ceremonially cleanse, to purify, and to counteract the terrible smell of

the corpse as it decomposed; like myrrh, this was very expensive and rare

8. "linen" (*othonion*) — a cloth made of very fine and extremely expensive materials that was fabricated primarily in Egypt; nobles were known to pay very high prices to have robes made for their wives from this material; this word suggests that Jesus was carefully laid in a large linen sheet of fine weave with specially prepared spices mingled between the folds of this high-priced garment in which Jesus' dead body was wrapped

9. "nigh" (*aggus*) — very close or very nearby

10. "new" (*kainos*) — fresh or unused

11. "hewn" (*laxeuo*) — to cut out or to polish; implies that it was a special, highly developed, refined tomb, or a tomb that was splendid and expensive; only royalty or wealthy individuals could afford to have their tombs carved out of a wall of stone

12. "laid" (*tithimi*) — to set, to deposit, to lay, to place, or to set in place; it portrays the careful and thoughtful placing of Jesus' body in its resting place inside the tomb

13. "beheld" (*theaomai*) — theater; to gaze upon, to fully see, or to look at intently; the women inspected the tomb and gazed on the dead body of Jesus to see that it had been honorably laid in place

14. "made sure" (*sphragidzo*) — a legal seal that was placed on documents, letters, possessions, or, in this case, a tomb; its purpose was to authenticate that the sealed item had been properly inspected before sealing and that all the contents were in order; as long as the seal remained unbroken, it guaranteed that the contents inside were safe and sound; in all probability, it was a string that was stretched across the stone at the entrance of the tomb, which was then sealed on both sides by Pilate's legal authorities

15. "watch" (*koustodia*) — a group of four Roman soldiers whose shifts changed every three hours; the changing shifts assured that the tomb would be guarded 24 hours a day by soldiers who were awake, attentive, and fully alert

SYNOPSIS

There are several facts about Jesus' burial that make it unique, but one of the most important things is the fact that not only was Jesus buried in a tomb, that tomb was also *sealed* by the government. But what would cause Roman officials to place a tamper-proof seal on the place where Jesus' body was laid? And why were two high-ranking Jewish leaders personally involved with both the preparation of Jesus' body and His burial? We'll answer these questions and more in this lesson.

The emphasis of this lesson:

Joseph of Arimathea and Nicodemus, two high-ranking Jewish leaders, meticulously prepared and cared for the body of Jesus after His death. They then lay Him in Joseph's personal, unused tomb. Jesus' body was handled and inspected by multiple people and confirmed dead — even by Roman officials. The tomb was then sealed and guarded.

A Holy Place of Preparation

Today, when people visit the Church of the Holy Sepulchre in Jerusalem, they will discover what remains of the traditional site of Golgotha as well as Jesus' tomb. But there is something else quite amazing that is found as one walks directly through the church's massive entrance. It is a large stone slab that once played an integral part in the story of Jesus' death and the preparation of His body for burial.

It is called The Stone of Anointing or The Stone of Unction, and it was discovered in approximately 326 AD by Emperor Constantine's mother, Helena, when she came to Jerusalem to identify biblical sites. An early tradition states this slab of stone was the location where Joseph of Arimathea and Nicodemus prepared Jesus' body for burial.

Who Was Joseph of Arimathea?

The Bible tells us that Pilate received a surprise visit from a high-ranking member of the Jewish Sanhedrin shortly after Jesus' death. We find this mentioned in Mark 15:42 and 43, which says:

> **And now when the even was come, because it was the preparation, that is, the day before the sabbath, Joseph of Arimathaea, an honourable counsellor, which also waited for the kingdom of God, came, and went in boldly unto Pilate, and craved the body of Jesus.**

Joseph of Arimathea was a high-ranking member of the Sanhedrin and a secret follower of Jesus. Arimathea was the city he was from, which was possibly located in the hill country of Ephraim a few miles northwest of Jerusalem. Moreover, the Bible says he was "honorable," which in Greek describes *people who have a good reputation; people who have a good standing in society;* or *people who are prominent, influential,* and *wealthy.*

Next, we see that he was a "counselor," which depicts a member of the Sanhedrin, and that is exactly who Joseph was. When he went to Pilate that day, Mark 15:43 says he *craved* the body of Jesus. The word "craved" means *to be adamant in requesting and demanding something,* and the word "body" in Greek describes *a dead body* and is often translated *as corpse.* The use of this word tells us that Jesus was dead by this time.

History informs us that it was the Roman custom to leave a body hanging on a cross until it rotted or until the vultures were finished picking away at it. Once the vultures were done, soldiers would take the body down and discard it in the wilderness where it was left to be eaten by wild dogs.

In contrast, Jews held the body in great awe because it was made in the image of God, and even when a person was executed by the Romans, they held the human body in such respect that they would not allow it to be picked apart by vultures or be eaten by dogs. Instead, Jews would remove a human body that had been hung or crucified just before sunset, taking it down so it could be prepared for burial.

The Bible goes on to say:

> **And Pilate marvelled if he were already dead: and calling unto him the centurion, he asked him whether he had been any while dead. And when he knew it of the centurion, he gave the body to Joseph.**
>
> **— Mark 15:44,45**

When Pilate wondered if Jesus was really already dead, he called for a centurion to verify it. If anyone could recognize a dead body, it would be a Roman Centurion. Once he confirmed that Jesus was indeed no longer alive, Jesus' body was taken down off the Cross and given to Joseph of Arimathea.

Nicodemus Joined Joseph
in Preparing Jesus' Body for Burial

It seems that at this point, Joseph was joined by another high-ranking member of the Sanhedrin who secretly admired and followed Jesus. His name was Nicodemus, and you may remember, he came to Jesus secretly and talked with Him in the middle of the night (*see* John 3:1-21). This is the same Nicodemus whom Jesus told, "…Except a man be born again, he cannot see the kingdom of God" (John 3:3). He had been following Jesus all this time, and now he reappeared at the time of Jesus' burial.

John 3:1 makes it clear that Nicodemus was "a man of the Pharisees." The fact that he was a Pharisee means he was earnestly waiting for the arrival of the Messiah, and he believed in the supernatural, which is what attracted him to Jesus' ministry — supernatural signs and wonders.

John 3:1 also tells us that Nicodemus was a "ruler of the Jews." The word "ruler" here means *chief one, ruler,* or *prince.* It denoted the rulers of local synagogues and members of the Sanhedrin who were the highest authorities in the land. And due to his high-ranking position, Nicodemus, like Joseph of Arimathea, was prominent, influential, and wealthy.

When we take into account both Matthew's gospel and John's gospel, we see two members of the Jewish Sanhedrin — Nicodemus and Joseph of Arimathea who were secret followers of Jesus — coming together after His crucifixion to gather Jesus' body and give Him a proper burial. The Bible says:

> **And there came also Nicodemus, which at the first came to Jesus by night, and brought a mixture of myrrh and aloes, about an hundred pound weight.**
> **— John 19:39**

The word "myrrh" in this passage describes *an expensive yellowish-brown, sweet-smelling gum resin that was obtained from a tree and had a bitter taste,* and it was chiefly used as a chemical for embalming the dead. This brings us to the word "aloes," which describes *a sweet-smelling fragrance derived from the juice pressed from the leaves of a tree found in the Middle East.* Aloes were used to ceremonially cleanse, to purify, and to counteract the terrible smell of a corpse as it decomposed.

Like myrrh, aloes were also very expensive and rare, and Scripture says Nicodemus brought along 100 pounds' worth. Only a rich man could have purchased such a massive combination of these costly, uncommon substances, which was actually far beyond what was needed to cleanse and embalm Jesus' body. Nevertheless, it was Nicodemus and Joseph's intention to fully cover the body of Jesus lavishly with these rare substances. They spared no expense in preparing His body for burial. This would be their last demonstration of love for Him.

Jesus Was Wrapped in a Robe of Royalty

John 19:40 goes on to say that Nicodemus and Joseph of Arimathea "...took they the body of Jesus, and wound it in linen clothes with the spices, as the manner of the Jews is to bury." After the Jews prepared the body of their loved ones who had died, they buried them naked with only a linen cloth wrapped around them. The Greek word for "linen" here describes *a cloth made of very fine and extremely expensive materials that was fabricated primarily in Egypt*. Nobles were known to pay very high prices to have robes made for their wives from this material.

The use of this word suggests that Jesus was carefully laid in a large linen sheet of fine weave with specially prepared spices mingled between the folds of this high-priced garment in which Jesus' dead body was wrapped. In other words, Joseph and Nicodemus gave meticulous care to Jesus' body. This is an amazing story of two men who dearly loved the Lord.

Keep in mind that during Jesus' ministry, it was very difficult for Joseph and Nicodemus to publicly follow Him because of their position. Yet, they followed Him to their fullest capability, and when Jesus died, they demonstrated their deep love for Him as they treated His dead body with tender care, using their personal wealth to bury Him with great honor. This was their last opportunity to show Jesus how much they loved Him, and they took full advantage of it.

Jesus had clearly taught, "For where your treasure is, there will your heart be also" (Matthew 6:21). When these two men used their wealth to bury Jesus, they illustrated that their hearts were with Him. He was their highest priority, so they invested their resources in showing their love for Him. They literally sowed their money into the ground when they bathed Jesus in 100 pounds of those rare substances, wrapped Him in an expensive cloth, and then buried Him in a rich man's tomb.

Jesus Was Buried in a Rich Man's Tomb

In the same way that Joseph of Arimathea and Nicodemus spared no expense to embalm and wrap Jesus' body for burial, they also spared no expense regarding the place of His burial. Here is what the apostle John wrote:

> **Now in the place where he was crucified there was a garden; and in the garden a new sepulchre, wherein was never man yet laid. There laid they Jesus therefore because of the Jews' preparation day; for the sepulchre was nigh at hand.**
> **—John 19:41,42**

The word "nigh" in this passage means *very close* or *very nearby*. History tells us that most crucifixions were performed along a roadside. Evidently this garden tomb was located in an orchard-like place, just down the road from where Jesus was crucified. And the fact that John 19:41 says He was laid in a "new" sepulchre, means it was a tomb that was *fresh or unused*. Indeed, no man had ever yet been laid there.

What is interesting is that Matthew, Mark, and Luke all record that this tomb belonged to Joseph of Arimathea. It was the custom of wealthy people in that day to prepare their grave for the future, which is what Joseph had done. This was the tomb he had made for his own burial. As a matter of fact, Matthew 27:60; Mark 15:46; and Luke 23:53 all note that the tomb was "hewn" out of rock or stone.

The Greek word for "hewn" means *to cut out or to polish*, and it implies that it was *a special, highly developed, refined tomb*, or *a tomb that was splendid and expensive*. Only royalty or wealthy individuals could afford to have their tombs carved out of a wall of stone.

Jesus being buried in a rich man's tomb was the fulfillment of what Isaiah had prophesied more than 700 years earlier. Isaiah 53:9 declared that the Messiah would be buried in a rich man's tomb, and that is exactly what we see happening in all four gospels.

Jesus Dead Body Was Carefully Inspected Again and Again

Looking once more at John 19:42, we read, "There laid they Jesus therefore because of the Jews' preparation day; for the sepulchre was nigh at hand." The word "laid" here means *to set*, *to deposit*, *to lay*, *to place*; *to set*; or *to set in place*. It portrays the careful and thoughtful placing of Jesus' body in its resting place inside the tomb.

Now stop and think about what was happening. Nicodemus and Joseph of Arimathea had been bathing Jesus' body in spices for hours and hours, washing all His wounds with aloes, washing away the blood, and pressing the myrrh into all the lacerations in His body. His blood would have been all over their hands.

If there had been a pulse or a heartbeat, they would have detected it, but there wasn't one — because Jesus was dead. Once they thoroughly inspected the place where they would lay Him, they placed Him in the tomb very carefully.

Luke 23:55 tells us, "And the women also, which came with him from Galilee, followed after, and beheld the sepulchre, and how his body was laid." The word "beheld" here is the Greek word for *a theater*, and it means *to gaze upon*, *to fully see*, or *to look at intently*. It tells us the women inspected the tomb and gazed on the dead body of Jesus to see that it had been honorably laid in place.

Mark's gospel says, "And Mary Magdalene and Mary the mother of Joses beheld where he was laid" (Mark 15:47). The word "beheld" here means these women took their time to make sure Jesus was properly laid there. Thus, it could be translated, "They *carefully contemplated* where he was laid."

Again, if Jesus had still been alive, those who buried Him would have certainly known it. They had spent substantial time preparing His body for burial. Then after His dead body was deposited into the tomb, the women gazed intensely at it to make sure He was treated with the greatest love and attention.

A Great Stone Door Sealed the Tomb

Matthew 27:60 says that with all this completed, "…he [Joseph of Arimathea] rolled a great stone to the door of the sepulchre, and departed." (*See also* Mark 15:46.) In his mind, everything was completed.

However, the chief priests feared Jesus' disciples would steal the body and claim that He had been resurrected. That is why they returned to Pilate and said:

...Sir, we remember that that deceiver said, while he was yet alive, After three days I will rise again. Command therefore that the sepulchre be made sure until the third day, lest his disciples come by night, and steal him away, and say unto the people, He is risen from the dead: so the last error shall be worse than the first.

— Matthew 27:63,64

Notice the words "made sure." In Greek, this describes *a legal seal that was placed on documents, letters, possessions*, or, *in this case, a tomb*. Its purpose was to authenticate that the sealed item had been properly inspected before sealing and that all the contents were in order; as long as the seal remained unbroken, it guaranteed that the contents inside were safe and sound. In all probability, this seal was a string that was stretched across the stone at the entrance of the tomb, which was then sealed on both sides by Pilate's legal authorities.

Before sealing the tomb, the Roman authorities were required to inspect the inside of it to see that the body of Jesus was in its place. This meant they had to roll back the stone and reopen the tomb so they could thoroughly investigate the contents inside. After guaranteeing that Jesus was dead and His corpse was where it was supposed to be, they rolled the stone back in place and sealed it with the official seal of the governor of Rome.

Four Groups of Roman Soldiers Guarded the Tomb

Once the tomb was inspected and sealed with Jesus' dead body inside, "Pilate said unto them, Ye have a watch: go your way, make it as sure as ye can" (Matthew 27:65).

The word "watch," which is also repeated in verse 66, is a Greek term describing *a group of four Roman soldiers whose shifts changed every three hours*. The changing shifts assured that the tomb would be guarded 24 hours a day by soldiers who were awake, attentive, and fully alert.

A better rendering of this verse would be, "Here — I'm giving you a set of soldiers; take them and guard the tomb."

Matthew 27:66 goes on to say, "So they went, and made the sepulchre sure, sealing the stone, and setting a watch." The chief priests hastened to the tomb with their government-issued soldiers and the special officers assigned to inspect the tomb before placing Pilate's seal upon it. After a full inspection was made, the stone was put back in place, and the soldiers stood guard to protect the tomb from anyone who would attempt to touch it or remove its contents.

Every three hours, new guards arrived to replace the old ones. These armed soldiers guarded the entrance to Jesus' tomb so firmly that no one would have been able to come near it. Again, the purpose of the seal was to authenticate Jesus' death. His body had been thoroughly inspected again, so there was no doubt that Jesus was indeed dead.

Jesus' Death Was Repeatedly Confirmed

Jesus' corpse was seen and even handled by numerous people. It was completely examined multiple times, and the process that was used by Romans proved beyond a doubt that Jesus was factually dead.

- The centurion made sure Jesus was dead and notified Pilate (Mark 15:44,45).

- Joseph of Arimathea and Nicodemus worked together to cleanse and embalm the body of Jesus. After handling His corpse for hours, they laid Him carefully inside the tomb (John 19:39-42).

- The women from Galilee examined Jesus' dead body and contemplated every aspect of the burial site to ensure everything was done properly (Luke 23:55).

- Rome's official officer ordered the stone rolled back, then went into the tomb and examined the body to verify that it was Jesus and that He was really dead.

- The chief priests and elders entered the tomb with Rome's official officer so they could look upon Jesus' dead body and put an end to their worries that He had somehow survived.

- Roman guards checked the contents of the tomb because they wanted to know for sure a body was there. They didn't want to be guarding an empty tomb that would later be used as a claim of resurrection (Matthew 27:65,66).

After all these inspections were complete, Rome's official officer ordered the stone to be rolled back in place. While the chief priests, elders, and Roman guards watched, he secured the site and sealed it shut with the seal of Pilate. Yet, regardless of all these efforts to secure the site and to keep Jesus inside the grave, it was impossible for death to hold Him.

On the morning of the third day, the power of God detonated inside that tomb, and Jesus came back to life! He was once really dead, but now He is fully alive!

When preaching on the day of Pentecost, Peter proclaimed, "God hath raised Him up, having loosed the pains of death: because it was not possible that he should be holden of it" (Acts 2:24). The power of God exploded inside that tomb, reconnecting Jesus' spirit with His dead body. God's power flooded His corpse with life, and Jesus arose and came out of that grave! This was no hoax or fabricated story.

In our next lesson, we will see what the Bible tells us about all the things that took place when Jesus was resurrected.

STUDY QUESTIONS

Study to shew thyself approved unto God, a workman that needeth not to be ashamed, rightly dividing the word of truth.
— 2 Timothy 2:15

1. Joseph of Arimathea was an important person who cared for Jesus' body at the time of His death. To help you better understand who he was and what he believed, read these gospel accounts, and in your own words, create a brief bio of this devoted disciple of Jesus: Matthew 27:57-60; Mark 15:42-46; Luke 23:50-55; and John 19:38-42.

2. Nicodemus was also a key player in the life and death of Jesus. Read these three passages from John's gospel and see what else you can learn about Nicodemus' unique position as a Jewish leader, his heart, and his faith: John 3:1-21; John 7:32-52; John 19:39-42.

PRACTICAL APPLICATION

But be ye doers of the word, and not hearers only, deceiving your own selves.
—James 1:22

1. What new details did you discover about what happened to Jesus in the hours *after* He died on the Cross and was placed in the tomb?

2. Had you ever stopped to think of all the hours it took to cleanse and embalm Jesus' body? If He was still alive, wouldn't they have detected it? Likewise, wouldn't the women have noticed any signs of life as they gazed intensely at Him? And what about the centurion at the Cross, the soldiers at the tomb, and the chief priests who all vehemently verified that Christ was dead. What do all these interactions with and investigations of Jesus' body say to you?

3. Imagine you were at the scene with Joseph of Arimathea, Nicodemus, Mary Magdalene, and Mary the mother of Joses, preparing Jesus' body for burial and carefully contemplating everything. What kind of thoughts might have run through your mind and what emotions might you have experienced?

LESSON 12

TOPIC
'Behold, He Is Risen!'

SCRIPTURES

1. **Matthew 28:1** — In the end of the sabbath, as it began to dawn toward the first day of the week, came Mary Magdalene and the other Mary to see the sepulchre.

2. **Luke 24:10** — It was Mary Magdalene and Joanna, and Mary the mother of James, and other women that were with them....

3. **Luke 8:3** — And Joanna the wife of Chuza Herod's steward....

4. **Luke 23:55,56** — And the women also, which came with him from Galilee, followed after, and beheld the sepulchre, and how his body was laid. And they returned, and prepared spices and ointments; and rested the sabbath day according to the commandment.

5. **Mark 16:2-4** — And very early in the morning the first day of the week, they came unto the sepulchre at the rising of the sun. And they said among themselves, Who shall roll us away the stone from the door of the sepulchre? And when they looked, they saw that the stone was rolled away: for it was very great.

6. **Matthew 28:2** — And, behold, there was a great earthquake: for the angel of the Lord descended from heaven, and came and rolled back the stone from the door, and sat upon it.

7. **Matthew 28:3** — His countenance was like lightning, and his raiment white as snow.

8. **Matthew 28:4** — And for fear of him the keepers did shake, and became as dead men.

9. **Luke 24:3** — And they entered in, and found not the body of the Lord Jesus.

10. **Mark 16:5** — And entering into the sepulchre, they saw a young man sitting on the right side, clothed in a long white garment; and they were affrighted.

11. **Luke 24:4** — And it came to pass, as they were much perplexed thereabout, behold, two men stood by them in shining garments.

12. **Luke 24:5-8** — And as they were afraid, and bowed down their faces to the earth, they said unto them, Why seek ye the living among the dead? He is not here, but is risen: remember how he spake unto you when he was yet in Galilee, saying, The Son of man must be delivered into the hands of sinful men, and be crucified, and the third day rise again. And they remembered his words.

13. **Mark 16:7** — But go your way, tell his disciples and Peter that he goeth before you into Galilee: there shall ye see him, as he said unto you.

14. **Matthew 28:8** — And they departed quickly from the sepulchre with fear and great joy; and did run to bring his disciples word.

15. **Mark 16:8** — And they went out quickly, and fled from the sepulchre....

16. **Luke 24:9-11** — And returned from the sepulchre, and told all these things unto the eleven, and to all the rest. It was Mary Magdalene and Joanna, and Mary the mother of James, and other women that were with them, which told these things unto the apostles. And their words seemed to them as idle tales, and they believed them not.

17. **John 20:2** — Then she [Mary Magdalene] runneth, and cometh to Simon Peter, and to the other disciple, whom Jesus loved, and saith unto them, They have taken away the Lord out of the sepulchre, and we know not where they have laid him.

18. **John 20:3,4** — Peter therefore went forth, and that other disciple, and came to the sepulchre. So they ran both together: and the other disciple did outrun Peter, and came first to the sepulchre.

19. **John 20:11** — But Mary stood without at the sepulchre weeping....
20. **John 20:5** — And he stooping down, and looking in, saw the linen clothes lying; yet went he not in.
21. **John 20:6,7** — Then cometh Simon Peter following him, and went into the sepulchre, and seeth the linen clothes lie, and the napkin, that was about his head, not lying with the linen clothes, but wrapped together in a place by itself.
22. **John 20:8** — Then went in also that other disciple, which came first to the sepulchre, and he saw, and believed.
23. **Luke 24:12** — Then arose Peter, and ran unto the sepulchre; and stooping down, he beheld the linen clothes laid by themselves, and departed, wondering in himself at that which was come to pass.

GREEK WORDS

1. "behold" (*idou*) — amazement, shock, and wonder
2. "great" (*mega*) — huge, massive, or enormous; depicts the magnitude of this event
3. "earthquake" (*seismos*) — a literal earthquake
4. "very" (*sphodra)* — very, exceedingly, or extremely
5. "great" (*mega*) — huge, massive, or enormous
6. "fear" (*phobos*) — in this case, a panic-stricken fear
7. "shake" (*seio*) — derived from the same word for an earthquake
8. "dead men" (*nekros*) — a corpse; dead people; corpses
9. "young man" (*neanikos*) — a young man who is filled with vigor and energy and who is in the prime of his life; this illustrates the vitality, strength, and ever-youthful appearance of angels
10. "clothed" (*periballo*) — pictures a garment draped about his shoulders, as a mighty warrior or ruler would be dressed
11. "garment" (*stole*) — a long, flowing robe that adorned royalty, commanders, kings, priests, and other people of high distinction
12. "perplexed" (*aporeo*) — to lose one's way; pictures one so confused that he can't figure out where he is, what he's doing, or what is happening around him; a person who is bewildered by surrounding events
13. "stood by" (*epistemi*) — to come upon suddenly; to take one by surprise; to burst upon the scene; to suddenly step up; or to unexpectedly appear

14. "shining" (*astrapto*) — something that shines or flashes like lightning
15. "idle tales" (*leros*) — nonsense, idle talk, babble, or delirium
16. "went forth" (exerchomai) — the tense indicates that their feet were moving before the conversation with the women concluded; when they heard that something had happened at the tomb, both men were on the move to get there as quickly as possible
17. "stooping down" (*parakupto*) — to peer into, to bend low to take a closer look, or to stoop down to see something better
18. "saw" (*blepo*) — to observe or to see; just enough of a glance to see the linen clothes lying there
19. "linen clothes" — expensive Egyptian-made garment in which Joseph of Arimathea and Nicodemus had buried Jesus
20. "seeth" (*theaomai*) — where we get our word theater; to fully see or fully observe, like a patron who carefully watches every act of a play at the theater
21. "napkin" (*soudarion*) — a napkin that could be used for wiping perspiration from one's face; also used in connection with a burial cloth that was gently placed upon the face of the dead at burial; Jesus' entire body was wrapped in a large white linen sheet, but His face was additionally covered with such a napkin in traditional Jewish burial style
22. "wrapped" (*entulisso*) — to neatly fold, to nicely arrange, or to arrange in an orderly fashion

SYNOPSIS

The story of Jesus' death, burial, and resurrection is not a fantasy, myth, or hoax. It is real, and the grave from which Jesus arose is found inside the Church of the Holy Sepulchre in Jerusalem. The site was rediscovered around 326 AD by Helena, the mother of Emperor Constantine, after interviewing the great distant relatives of those who had lived around the time of Christ.

Three days after Jesus' dead body had been sealed in the tomb by Roman authorities and a rotating regiment of soldiers were keeping watch, the unimaginable and unprecedented took place. The power of God exploded inside that tomb, flooding with life the broken body of Jesus and physically resurrecting Him from the dead! The stone was rolled away, the earth violently shook, and the world has never been the same since!

The emphasis of this lesson:

The first people to go to the tomb on the morning of Jesus' resurrection were Mary Magdalene, Joanna, and a group of other women. They encountered several angels in dazzling clothes, both outside and inside the tomb. These women became the first evangelists to tell others that the tomb was empty and Christ had risen. Then Peter and John went to the tomb to see for themselves the evidence of this miraculous event.

The First Responders on the Scene

It seems that Jesus was resurrected sometime between the close of the Sabbath sunset on Saturday evening and before the first visitors came to the tomb early on Sunday morning. A careful examination of the gospels of Matthew, Mark, Luke, and John enables us to piece together in a somewhat chronological order all the events that took place on the morning of the resurrection, including those who were the first people to arrive on the scene.

Beginning in Matthew 28:1, the Bible says:

> **In the end of the sabbath, as it began to dawn toward the first day of the week, came Mary Magdalene and the other Mary to see the sepulchre.**

Looking at Luke 24:10, we see that others also visited the tomb.

> **It was Mary Magdalene and Joanna, and Mary the mother of James, and other women that were with them.**

Mary Magdalene was the woman from whom Jesus cast out multiple evil spirits, and according to Luke 8:3, Joanna was the wife of Chuza, Herod's steward. Apparently, Joanna was a very wealthy woman who had financially supported Jesus' ministry.

In Luke 23:55 and 56, we see that all these women were at the tomb when Nicodemus and Joseph of Arimathea had finished preparing Jesus' body and had laid Him inside. Hence, they were also there when the stone was first rolled into place over the mouth of the grave.

These women had no way of knowing that the chief priests had gone to Pilate the day after Jesus was buried to request a watch of Roman soldiers to guard the tomb and an official from the Roman court to "seal" the tomb. They were at home, preparing spices and ointments to return after the Sabbath to anoint Jesus' dead body.

While they prepared, the tomb was being officially inspected and sealed shut, and Roman soldiers had been ordered to guard the tomb 24 hours a day. Had the women known that the tomb was legally sealed and couldn't be opened, they wouldn't have returned to the tomb, for it was legally impossible for them to request the stone to be removed.

The Massive Stone Had Been Removed

Without question, how to remove the stone from the tomb's entrance was at the forefront of the women's minds. This is confirmed in Mark's gospel, which says:

> **And very early in the morning the first day of the week, they came unto the sepulchre at the rising of the sun. And they said among themselves, Who shall roll us away the stone from the door of the sepulchre? And when they looked, they saw that the stone was rolled away: for it was very great.**
> **— Mark 16:2-4**

Much to the women's surprise, the huge stone had already been removed before they arrived at the tomb. It seems that something supernatural had happened. Turning our attention back to Matthew's account, we read, "And, behold, there was a great earthquake…" (Matthew 28:2).

The word "behold" in Greek expresses *shock*, *amazement*, and *wonder*. Its use here is the equivalent of Matthew saying, "Wow! Can you believe it? Whew! Listen to the amazing thing that happened next. There was an earthquake…."

It is important to note that this "earthquake" was *a literal earthquake*, and it didn't occur when the women approached the tomb; it happened simultaneously with the moment of Jesus' resurrection. And the earthquake was "great," which is the Greek word for *huge*, *massive*, or *enormous*, and depicts the magnitude of this event. Just as creation shook when its Creator died on the Cross, the earth exploded with joy at the resurrection of Jesus!

Again, Mark 16:4 tells us that when the women arrived at the tomb, "…They saw that the stone was rolled away: for it was very great." The word "very" means *very, exceedingly*, or *extremely*, and the word "great" means *huge, massive*, or *enormous*. This was no normal stone. The authorities had placed an extremely, exceedingly massive stone in front of the entrance to Jesus' tomb so that it would remain closed. Yet when the women arrived, it had been removed!

The Soldiers Were Paralyzed With Fear at the Sight of the Angels

Let's take a quick look at what happened at the grave site just before the women arrived. Matthew 28:2 and 3 says, "…For the angel of the Lord descended from heaven, and came and rolled back the stone from the door, and sat upon it. His countenance was like lightning, and his raiment white as snow."

The word "sat" in verse 2 literally means *to sit down.* The fact that the angel could sit on top of such a huge stone may denote his immense size. It seems he was so huge that he could sit on top of the enormous stone as if it were a chair. If this was the case, the removal of the stone would have been a simple feat.

In addition to being extremely strong, the angel's "…countenance was like lightning, and his raiment white as snow" (Matthew 28:3). The size, power, and brilliance of this angel explains the guards' response. The Bible says, "And for fear of him the keepers did shake, and became as dead men" (Matthew 28:4).

The Greek word for "fear" in this case is the word *phobos,* which describes *a panic-stricken fear,* and the word "shake" is derived from the same Greek word for *earthquake.* So just as the earth shook and quaked, these guards trembled at the sight of the powerful angel.

The guards also became as "dead men." The original Greek term here describes *a corpse* or *dead people.* When the soldiers witnessed the earthquake and saw the angel appear and roll away the massive stone, they became like lifeless corpses, paralyzed by fear and unable to move. When they regained composure and were finally able to move again, these guards fled the scene! This is the state in which the group of women found the grave site.

Angels, Angels Everywhere!

Arriving at the tomb and astonished that the stone had been rolled away, the women, "…entered in, and found not the body of the Lord Jesus." So after the women saw the huge angel sitting on the stone, they made their way past him and entered the tomb. Mark then adds, "And entering into the sepulchre, they saw a young man sitting on the right side, clothed in a long white garment; and they were affrighted" (Mark 16:5).

Instead of finding Jesus' body, the women encountered "a young man sitting on the right side." This was another angel whose appearance was like a "young man," a phrase derived from the Greek that describes *a young man who is filled with vigor and energy and who is in the prime of his life.* This illustrates the vitality, strength, and ever-youthful appearance of angels.

According to Mark 16:5, this angel was "clothed in a long white garment" (Mark 16:5). The Greek word for "clothed" pictures *a garment draped about his shoulders, as a mighty warrior or ruler would be dressed.* And the word "garment" describes *a long, flowing robe that adorned royalty, commanders, kings, priests, and other people of high distinction.*

When these women stood in the empty tomb and saw this young warrior angel, they were afraid, and Luke 24:4 says, "…They were much perplexed thereabout…." The word "perplexed" here means *to lose one's way* and pictures *one so confused that he can't figure out where he is, what he's doing, or what is happening around him.* It describes *someone who is totally bewildered by surrounding events.*

It really is no surprise that the women were *perplexed.* They came to the tomb expecting to find the huge stone blocking the entrance, but the stone had been removed. Sitting on top of the stone was a large angel, and as they went inside the tomb, they expected to see Jesus' body, but His body was missing. Then, suddenly, they looked over to the right side of the tomb and saw a second angel dressed in a long, white robe like that of a warrior, ruler, priest, or king.

The Angels Talked With the Women

With their heads swirling from all they were seeing, "…behold, two men stood by them in shining garments" (Luke 24:4). The phrase "stood by" in Greek means *to come upon suddenly; to take one by surprise; to burst upon the scene; to suddenly step up;* or *to unexpectedly appear.* Suddenly, the women saw two angels standing by them inside the tomb in "shining garments." The word "shining" describes *something that shines or flashes like lightning.*

How did the women respond to the sudden appearance of two more angels? The Bible says:

> **And as they were afraid, and bowed down their faces to the earth, they [the angels] said unto them, Why seek ye the living among the dead? He is not here, but is risen: remember how he spake unto you when he was yet in Galilee, saying, The Son of man must be delivered into the hands of sinful men, and be crucified, and the third day rise again. And they remembered his words.**
>
> — Luke 24:5-8

Here, the angels clearly stated Jesus was not dead — and that is still the case today. *He is alive!* He is among the living. He rose from the grave just as He said He would. The angels' words suddenly jolted the memory of the women who then remembered what Jesus had said.

Turning to Mark's gospel, we see that the angels then gave the women these instructions:

> **But go your way, tell his disciples and Peter that he goeth before you into Galilee: there shall ye see him, as he said unto you.**
> — Mark 16:7

This group of women — the first of Jesus' followers to visit the tomb — were assigned the task of telling the disciples that Jesus had come back to life and that the Lord Himself would meet them in Galilee.

Women Were the First
To Preach Christ's Resurrection

When you stop and think about it, *women were the first preachers of the Gospel.* They were the very first to announce the Good News — that Jesus who had died on the Cross had risen from the dead, defeating death, hell, and the grave.

Matthew 28:8 says, "And they [the women] departed quickly from the sepulchre with fear and great joy; and did run to bring his disciples word."

Mark 16:8 states, "And they went out quickly, and fled from the sepulchre...."

Luke 24:9 and 10 says, "[The women] returned from the sepulchre, and told all these things unto the eleven, and to all the rest. It was Mary

Magdalene and Joanna, and Mary the mother of James, and other women that were with them, which told these things unto the apostles."

Can you imagine how flustered these women must have been as they tried to tell the apostles what they had seen and heard that morning? Somehow, they managed to get the words out and share the news of Jesus' resurrection, but when they did, "...their words seemed to them as idle tales, and they believed them not" (Luke 24:11).

The phrase "idle tales" describes *nonsense, idle talk, babble, or delirium*. No doubt, the women sounded confused, and their presentation wasn't extremely clear. However, even though they seemed to be babbling and speaking nonsense, their words were all that was needed to spark an interest in some of the disciples and compel them to get up and go find out about Jesus themselves.

Upon Hearing the Women's Testimony Peter and John Ran to the Tomb

Writing about this same event, the apostle John focused on Mary Magdalene's experience, saying:

Then she runneth, and cometh to Simon Peter, and to the other disciple, whom Jesus loved, and saith unto them, They have taken away the Lord out of the sepulchre, and we know not where they have laid him. Peter therefore went forth, and that other disciple, and came to the sepulchre. So they ran both together: and the other disciple did outrun Peter, and came first to the sepulchre.

— John 20:2-4

Here we see the women's words stirred enough interest in Peter and John — who identifies himself as "the other disciple" — to make them get up and go find out for themselves about Jesus! It's interesting to note that the other apostles just watched as Peter and John took off running. Instead of joining them, the apostles stayed behind, probably to discuss what they had just heard and to debate what it meant.

When the Bible says Peter and John "went forth," the tense here indicates that *their feet were moving before the conversation with the women concluded.* Hence, when they heard that something had happened at the tomb, both men were on the move to get there as quickly as possible.

Because Peter and John raced to the garden, they experienced something the other apostles missed by staying home. It is a fact that if you want to experience Jesus Christ and His power, you must get up from where you are and start moving in His direction just like Peter and John did.

John Was an Eyewitness to the Empty Tomb and Its Contents

According to John 20:4, John outran Peter and made it to the tomb first. Scripture then says:

> **And he stooping down, and looking in, saw the linen clothes lying; yet went he not in.**
> — **John 20:5**

Notice the words "stooping down." In Greek, this means *to peer into, to bend low to take a closer look*, or *to stoop down to see something better*. To get a better look at what was inside the tomb, John bent down low and "saw the linen clothes." The word "saw" means *to observe* or *to see*. John got just enough of a glance to see the linen clothes lying there, and the Greek meaning of the words "linen clothes" is *an expensive Egyptian-made garment* — the kind of garment in which Joseph of Arimathea and Nicodemus had buried Jesus.

If Jesus' body had been stolen, as the religious leaders alleged, whoever took Him would have also taken this expensive garment. But John was an eyewitness that these linen clothes had been left lying in the tomb.

It is interesting to note that John didn't go inside the tomb when he first arrived (*see* John 20:5). Traditionally, the Jews in Jesus' time held great respect for tombs and graves, which explains why John was hesitant to enter. It is also possible that he observed Pilate's Roman seal had been broken and realized that it looked like an unlawful entry had occurred.

Peter Was Also an Eyewitness, Observing the 'Linen Clothes' and 'Napkin'

But regardless of why John hesitated, Peter did not hesitate — he barged right into the tomb to check it out for himself. That is what we find in John 20:6 and 7:

Then cometh Simon Peter following him, and went into the sepulchre, and seeth the linen clothes lie, and the napkin, that was about his head, not lying with the linen clothes, but wrapped together in a place by itself.

According to this verse, Peter also saw the linen clothes and the napkin. In Greek, the word "seeth" found in John 20:6 is where we get our word *theater*. It means *to fully see or fully observe, like a patron who carefully watches every act of a play at the theater.*

The use of this word indicates Peter was taking it all in — fully inspecting and observing the interior of the tomb. He looked over every nook and cranny, paying special attention to the linen clothes and how the *napkin* was left.

This word "napkin" depicts *a napkin that could be used for wiping perspiration from one's face*, but it was also used in connection with *a burial cloth that was gently placed upon the face of the dead at burial*. Jesus' entire body had been wrapped in a large white linen sheet, but His face was additionally covered with such a napkin in traditional Jewish burial style.

Specifically, the Bible says this napkin was "wrapped together in a place by itself" (John 20:7). The meaning of the word "wrapped" here is *to neatly fold; to nicely arrange;* or *to arrange in an orderly fashion.* The inclusion of this word lets us know that when Jesus was raised back to life, He was calm and completely in control of His faculties. He removed the expensive burial cloth from His body and removed the burial napkin from His face. Sitting in an upright position, He neatly folded the burial napkin and gently laid it down to one side, separate from the linen clothes He probably laid down on His other side.

John Left the Tomb Believing… Peter Left the Tomb Wondering

The Bible goes on to say, "Then went in also that other disciple, which came first to the sepulchre, and he saw, and believed" (John 20:8). This "other disciple" was John. When John went into the tomb and took in the full weight of Jesus' body missing and saw the linen clothes and napkin left behind, he believed!

Peter's response was somewhat different from John's response. After he ran to the Sepulchre, stooped down low, and saw the linen clothes, he, "…departed, wondering in himself at that which was come to pass" (Luke 24:12). So, while John left the tomb *believing* Jesus was alive, Peter left *wondering* what it all meant.

- How in the world would it be possible to be in the very room where Jesus' dead body had lain, to see the neatly folded napkin, to recognize the spot where He sat upright between those garments, and to still not be able to figure out that something miraculous had taken place with Jesus?

Friend, the truth is Jesus is alive! His resurrection was not merely a philosophical renaissance of His ideas and teachings — He was literally raised from the dead!

Did you notice the multitude of events that took place the morning of Jesus' resurrection? There was an earthquake and multiple angelic appearances inside and outside the tomb. Likewise, a group of women were at the tomb, and their testimony spurred Peter and John to go to the tomb where they all saw with their own eyes that Jesus' body was gone, and all that remained was the expensive linen clothes and the folded napkin that covered His face.

In our next lesson, you'll learn about the many eyewitnesses of Jesus' resurrection.

STUDY QUESTIONS

Study to shew thyself approved unto God, a workman that needeth not to be ashamed, rightly dividing the word of truth.
— 2 Timothy 2:15

1. Matthew, Mark, Luke, and John all document many amazing things that took place in and around the tomb of Jesus. What new insights did you learn about these events and the people who were present the morning of the resurrection?

2. Immediately after Jesus surrendered His spirit and died, the veil in the Temple in Jerusalem was ripped in two from top to bottom. What other extraordinary events took place that are recorded in Matthew 27:52-54? If you had been in Jerusalem and had witnessed these events, what might have been your response?

PRACTICAL APPLICATION

But be ye doers of the word, and not hearers only,
deceiving your own selves.
— James 1:22

1. As you ponder the multitude of happenings the morning of Jesus' resurrection — the earthquake, the multiple angelic appearances, the testimony of the women, and the eyewitness accounts of John and Peter — what is your reaction?

2. Some skeptics who question the validity of Scripture may look at the differences in the gospel accounts (i.e. the number of angels and the places they appeared on resurrection morning) as "proof" the Bible cannot be trusted. Others point to the differences in each telling of the events as proof the testimonies are factual. How do you view these discrepancies in the gospels?

3. Like Mary Magdalene and the other women, telling others about your supernatural encounter with God can be hard to put into words and it isn't always received. Pray and ask the Holy Spirit to empower you to share the truth as best you can and to trust Him to stir a hunger in the heart of the hearers and to continue dealing with them long after you're done speaking.

LESSON 13

TOPIC

Eyewitnesses of Jesus' Resurrection

SCRIPTURES

1. **Mark 16:6** — And he saith unto them, Be not affrighted: Ye seek Jesus of Nazareth, which was crucified: he is risen; he is not here: behold the place where they laid him.

2. **Luke 24:6** — He is not here, but is risen....

3. **John 20:11,12** — But Mary stood without at the sepulchre weeping: and as she wept, she stooped down, and looked into the sepulchre, And seeth two angels in white sitting, the one at the head, and the other at the feet, where the body of Jesus had lain.

4. **John 20:13,14** — And they say unto her, Woman, why weepest thou? She saith unto them, Because they have taken away my Lord, and I know not where they have laid him. And when she had thus said, she turned herself back, and saw Jesus standing, and knew not that it was Jesus.

5. **John 20:15** — Jesus saith unto her, Woman, why weepest thou? whom seekest thou? She, supposing him to be the gardener, saith unto him, Sir, if thou have borne him hence, tell me where thou hast laid him, and I will take him away.

6. **John 20:16** — Jesus saith unto her, Mary. She turned herself, and saith unto him, Rabboni; which is to say, Master.

7. **John 20:17** — …Touch me not; for I am not yet ascended unto my Father: but go to my brethren, and say unto them, I ascend unto my Father, and your Father; and to my God, and your God.

8. **John 20:18** — Mary Magdalene came and told the disciples that she had seen the Lord, and that he had spoken these things unto her.

9. **Luke 24:30,31** — And it came to pass, as he sat at meat with them, he took bread, and blessed it, and brake, and gave to them. And their eyes were opened, and they knew him; and he vanished out of their sight.

10. **John 20:19** — Then the same day at evening, being the first day of the week, when the doors were shut where the disciples were assembled for fear of the Jews....

11. **Matthew 28:11-15** — Now when they were going, behold, some of the watch came into the city, and shewed unto the chief priests all the things that were done. And when they were assembled with the elders, and had taken counsel, they gave large money unto the soldiers, Saying, Say ye, His disciples came by night, and stole him away while we slept. And if this come to the governor's ears, we will persuade him, and secure you. So they took the money, and did as they were taught: and this saying is commonly reported among the Jews until this day.

12. **John 20:19** — Then the same day at evening, being the first day of the week, when the doors were shut where the disciples were assembled for fear of the Jews, came Jesus and stood in the midst, and saith unto them, Peace be unto you.

13. **Luke 24:37** — But they were terrified and affrighted, and supposed that they had seen a spirit.

14. **Luke 24:38,39** — And he said unto them, Why are ye troubled? and why do thoughts arise in your hearts? Behold my hands and my feet, that it is I myself: handle me, and see; for a spirit hath not flesh and bones, as ye see me have.

15. **Luke 24:41-43** — And while they yet believed not for joy, and wondered, he said unto them, Have ye here any meat? And they gave him a piece of a broiled fish, and of an honeycomb. And he took it, and did eat before them.

16. **John 20:25** — The other disciples therefore said unto him, We have seen the Lord. But he said unto them, Except I shall see in his hands the print of the nails, and put my finger into the print of the nails, and thrust my hand into his side, I will not believe.

17. **John 20:26,27** — And after eight days again his disciples were within, and Thomas with them: Then came Jesus, the doors being shut, and stood in the midst, and said, Peace be unto you. Then saith he to Thomas, Reach hither thy finger, and behold my hands; and reach hither thy hand, and thrust it into my side: and be not faithless, but believing.

18. **John 21:14** — This is now the third time that Jesus shewed himself to his disciples, after that he was risen from the dead.

19. **Matthew 28:18-20** — And Jesus came and spake unto them, saying, All power is given unto me in heaven and in earth. Go ye therefore, and teach all nations, baptizing them in the name of the Father, and of the Son, and of the Holy Ghost: teaching them to observe all things whatsoever I have commanded you: and, lo, I am with you always, even unto the end of the world. Amen.

20. **1 Corinthians 15:5-7** — And that he was seen of Cephas, then of the twelve: after that, he was seen of above five hundred brethren at once; of whom the greater part remain unto this present, but some are fallen asleep. After that, he was seen of James; then of all the apostles.

21. **Acts 1:3** — …He shewed himself alive after his passion by many infallible proofs, being seen of them forty days, and speaking of the things pertaining to the kingdom of God.

GREEK WORDS

1. "stooped down" (*parakupto*) — to peer into, to bend low to take a closer look, or to stoop down to see something better

2. "seeth" (*theaomai*) — fixed her eyes on the angels and determined to look them over, taking in the whole experience

3. "in white" (*en leukos*) — a lightning-bright appearance

4. "doors" (*thura*) — a large and solid door

5. "shut" (*kleio*) — locked; doors of this kind were usually locked with a heavy bolt that slid through rings attached to the door and the frame — like the deadbolts we use in doors today, only heavier; such a door would be difficult, if not impossible, to break down

6. "handle me" (*psilaphao*) — to touch, to squeeze, or to feel; thus, Jesus gave the disciples permission to examine His resurrected body to see that it was a real body and not a spirit

SYNOPSIS

Again and again, God's Word declares, "…On the testimony of two or three witnesses every matter may be confirmed" (Matthew 18:16 *NASB*). This truth is repeated in Deuteronomy 19:15; Matthew 18:16; Second Corinthians 13:1; First Timothy 5:19; and Hebrews 10:28.

Throughout the New Testament and even in secular records, there are documented eyewitness reports of people who testified of seeing Jesus alive after He was executed by crucifixion. Indeed, one account states that a group of more than 500 people saw Jesus all at the same time, and He was fully alive! The fact that we have exceedingly more than two or three witnesses that physically saw Jesus over the course of 40 days is solid proof that He was resurrected, and He is alive today!

The emphasis of this lesson:

Mary Magdalene was the first to encounter Jesus in His resurrected body. Along with Mary, numerous other eyewitnesses testified of seeing Jesus alive after He had been crucified, including His 11 disciples on multiple occasions, the Roman guards, and a crowd of more than 500 people.

Mary Magdalene and the Women With Her Encountered Several Angels on Resurrection Day

In our previous lesson, we saw that Peter and John came running to Jesus' tomb after hearing the women's report that His body was no longer there.

Mary Magdalene followed them back to the site, and once the men left, she remained outside the tomb weeping.

Remember, Mary and a group of devoted women had already been to the tomb earlier that morning, and they had seen the huge stone rolled back and an angel sitting on top of it. When they went inside the tomb, they encountered another angel who had the appearance of a vibrant young man:

> **And he saith unto them, Be not affrighted: Ye seek Jesus of Nazareth, which was crucified: he is risen; he is not here: behold the place where they laid him.**
>
> **— Mark 16:6**

At that point, Mary and those with her were confused and perplexed by all they were seeing. Just as they were trying to gather themselves, "…two men stood by them in shining garments: And as they were afraid, and bowed down their faces to the earth, they said unto them, Why seek ye the living among the dead? He is not here, but is risen…" (Luke 24:4-6).

When Mary Magdalene returned to Jesus' tomb with Peter and John, the disciples went back to their home shortly thereafter. Scripture goes on to say:

> **But Mary stood without at the sepulchre weeping: and as she wept, she stooped down, and looked into the sepulchre, and seeth two angels in white sitting, the one at the head, and the other at the feet, where the body of Jesus had lain.**
>
> **— John 20:11,12**

Note that the tense of the word "weeping" is *ongoing*, which means she was *continually weeping*, indicating that she was extremely troubled about the inexplicable events that were happening. Most of all, she wanted to know what had happened to Jesus.

To learn more, Mary "stooped down, and looked into the sepulchre" (John 20:11). The words "stooped down" are a translation of a Greek phrase meaning *to peer into, to bend low to take a closer look*, or *to stoop down to see something better*. Verse 12 says she then "seeth two angels in white." The word "seeth" means that she *fixed her eyes on the angels and determined to look them over, taking in the whole experience*.

These angels were dressed "in white," which in Greek describes *a lightning-bright appearance*. This is the same apparel we saw the angels wearing in Luke 24:4. They all wore the same type of robe — a long, flowing regal robe like those worn by warriors, kings, priests, or any other person of great power and authority.

Mary visibly studied every single detail of the angels she saw in the tomb. In this instance, one angel was positioned at either end of where Jesus' body had once lain. In between these angels, Mary could see the empty place where she had personally viewed Jesus several days earlier. Now Mary saw the same spot, but Jesus' body was no longer there.

Mary Encountered the Risen Christ Himself!

As Mary stood at the entrance of the tomb continuing to weep, the angels said to her:

> ...Woman, why weepest thou? She saith unto them, Because they have taken away my Lord, and I know not where they have laid him. And when she had thus said, she turned herself back, and saw Jesus standing, and knew not that it was Jesus.
> — John 20:13,14

Keep in mind, the last image Mary had of Jesus was after He had been beaten beyond recognition by the Roman scourge and crucified on the Cross. It was His mangled form she envisioned in her mind. The reason she couldn't readily recognize Jesus is because He was in His glorified body, and His physical appearance had changed. In that tender moment, Jesus Himself spoke to Mary and said:

> ...Woman, why weepest thou? whom seekest thou? She, supposing him to be the gardener, saith unto him, Sir, if thou have borne him hence, tell me where thou hast laid him, and I will take him away.
> — John 20:15

At that very moment...

> Jesus saith unto her, *Mary*. She turned herself, and saith unto him, Rabboni; which is to say, Master.
> — John 20:16

Although Jesus certainly looked different in His glorified body, His voice was the same. Mary Magdalene knew the Master's voice! When He called her name, it was like music to her ears. The instant her eyes were opened, and she knew it was Jesus, she reached out to cling to Him with her hands, but Jesus said:

> ...Touch me not; for I am not yet ascended to my Father: but go to my brethren, and say unto them, I ascend unto my Father, and your Father; and to my God, and your God. Mary Magdalene came and told the disciples that she had seen the Lord, and that he had spoken these things unto her.
> — John 20:17,18

Here we see that Mary became the first person to clearly declare the good news of Jesus' resurrection! Her passionate and persistent devotion to Christ enabled her to see Him and hear Him before anyone else did.

There Were Multiple Eyewitness Accounts That Jesus Rose From the Dead

A careful study of the New Testament reveals that there were numerous eyewitness accounts that Jesus had risen from the dead. For example, on Resurrection Day, Jesus appeared to the disciples at various times and places, which is truly amazing because it was physically impossible for Him to be at so many different places in one day. But the record of all those appearances reveals that Jesus' glorified body didn't have the same limitations His earthly body possessed before His resurrection and glorification.

In His glorified condition, Jesus was able to appear, disappear, travel great distances, and even supernaturally pass through the solid walls and locked doors of a house and visit with people. Consider all these various appearances and the people to whom Jesus revealed Himself:

Jesus appeared to Mary Magdalene.

This happened outside of the garden tomb on the day He was resurrected (*see* John 20:14-17).

Jesus appeared to two disciples on their way to the city of Emmaus.

As two of Jesus' disciples walked from Jerusalem to Emmaus, they ran into Jesus, but they didn't recognize Him (*see* Luke 24:13-31). When the three men sat down to eat together, Jesus blessed the food, broke it, and gave it to the two disciples. Instantly their eyes were open, and they recognized it was the Lord — just as He "...vanished out of their sight" (Luke 24:31).

Jesus appeared to His disciples behind closed doors.

John 20:19 says, "Then the same day at evening, being the first day of the week, when the doors were shut where the disciples were assembled for fear of the Jews, came Jesus and stood in the midst, and saith unto them, Peace be unto you."

The word "door" in Greek describes *a large and solid door*, and the verse says it was "shut." This word "shut" means *locked*. Doors of this kind were usually locked with a heavy bolt that slid through rings attached to the door and the frame — like the deadbolts we use in doors today, only heavier. Such a door would be difficult, if not impossible, to break down.

Jesus literally walked right through that door and the walls of that room, right where the 11 disciples were gathered, and miraculously stood in front of them. This was His first appearance to the disciples collectively.

Jesus appeared to the Roman soldiers who were guarding His tomb.

On the morning of Jesus resurrection, the power of God detonated inside the tomb, and Jesus came back to life! The ground quaked as the angel rolled away the massive stone, and Jesus became visible to all the guards on duty.

The Bible says the Roman guards "…did shake, and became as dead men" (Matthew 28:4). We saw in Lesson 12 that the words "dead men" means these soldiers were so paralyzed with fear they became like *lifeless corpses* when Jesus was resurrected.

Once the Roman guards regained their composure and were able to move again, "…some of the watch came into the city, and shewed unto the chief priests all the things that were done" (Matthew 28:11). The word "watch" here refers to the *rotating regiment of soldiers* assigned to guard Jesus' tomb 24 hours a day.

'Fake News' Was Released by the Pharisees About What Had Happened to Jesus

These guards had witnessed the resurrection and knew Jesus had walked out of the tomb alive! That is what they came into the city to tell the chief priests. But to prevent the people of Israel from knowing the truth of Jesus' resurrection, the religious leaders bribed the soldiers to keep their mouths shut — and tell a lie about what happened. Here is what the Bible says:

> **And when they [the chief priests] were assembled with the elders, and had taken counsel, they gave large money unto the soldiers, saying, Say ye, His disciples came by night, and stole him away while we slept.**
> **— Matthew 28:12,13**

If the soldiers had admitted that they were sleeping on the job, that was a punishable offense, and they would have been killed. The Jewish leaders knew that, which is why they told the soldiers:

> **And if this come to the governor's ears, we will persuade him, and secure you. So they [the soldiers] took the money, and did as they were taught: and this saying is commonly reported among the Jews until this day.**
> **— Matthew 28:14,15**

With the soldiers adequately bribed and on board with spinning the story, the chief priests and elders began to spread their fabricated tale that the soldiers fell asleep, and while they slept, the disciples came and stole Jesus' body.

But to steal Jesus' body, the disciples would have had to overpower the Roman guards or creep past them as they slept. This would be deemed a terrible dishonor to the guards' reputation. Moreover, if the disciples were caught, they'd be put to death for this action because breaking the governor's seal to reopen that tomb would be a capital offense that required the death sentence. Nevertheless, this was the fable that was perpetuated among the Jews.

Jesus Told the Disciples To 'Handle' His Resurrected Body

Although the doors were sealed tight on the evening of the resurrection, Jesus passed right through them and the walls and appeared in the midst of the disciples. Again, John 20:19 says, "Then the same day at evening, being the first day of the week, when the doors were shut where the disciples were assembled for fear of the Jews, came Jesus and stood in the midst, and saith unto them, Peace be unto you."

When we go to Luke's gospel, we see more of what happened once Jesus was inside. The Bible says:

> **But they were terrified and affrighted, and supposed that they had seen a spirit. And he said unto them, Why are ye troubled? and why do thoughts arise in your hearts? Behold my hands and my feet, that it is I myself: handle me, and see; for a spirit hath not flesh and bones, as ye see me have.**
> **— Luke 24:37-39**

Isn't it interesting that Jesus actually said to His disciples, "Handle me." In Greek, this means *to touch, to squeeze, or to feel*. Thus, Jesus gave His closest friends permission to examine His resurrected body to see that it was a real body and not a spirit. The Bible goes on to say:

> **And while they yet believed not for joy, and wondered, he said unto them, Have ye here any meat? And they gave him a piece of a broiled fish, and of an honeycomb. And he took it, and did eat before them.**
> **— Luke 24:41-43**

The reason Jesus ate food right in front of His disciples was to show them He was real and not a ghost. Spirits don't eat — but people do. Jesus was a real person in His resurrected body, and that is what He was demonstrating.

Thomas was not there the first time Jesus passed through solid matter and entered the upper room, so the other disciples told him what had happened. Upon hearing their report, Thomas replied:

> **...Except I shall see in his hands the print of the nails, and put my finger into the print of the nails, and thrust my hand into his side, I will not believe. And after eight days again his disciples were within, and Thomas with them: then came Jesus, the doors being shut, and stood in the midst, and said, Peace be unto you. Then saith he to Thomas, Reach hither thy finger, and behold my hands; and reach hither thy hand, and thrust it into my side: and be not faithless, but believing.**
> **— John 20:25-27**

Thomas ended up getting exactly the proof he felt he needed in order to believe. Jesus allowed Thomas to touch His nail-scarred hands and feel the wound in His side then commanded him to "be not faithless, but believing" (v. 27).

Jesus Appeared to Disciples at the Sea of Tiberias

As John wrapped up Chapter 20, he wrote that Jesus did many other signs in the presence of His disciples, which he did not detail in his book (v. 30). Meanwhile, the disciples continued to stick together, and on another occasion when seven of the disciples were at the Sea of Tiberias, Jesus appeared to them once again. This would be the third "Jesus sighting" by the disciples. John wrote:

> **There were together Simon Peter, and Thomas called Didymus, and Nathanael of Cana in Galilee, and the sons of Zebedee, and two other of his disciples. Simon Peter saith unto them, I go a fishing. They say unto him, We also go with thee. They went forth, and entered into a ship immediately; and that night they caught nothing. But when the morning was now come, Jesus stood on the shore: but the disciples knew not that it was Jesus. Then Jesus saith unto them, Children, have ye any meat? They answered him, No. And he said unto them, Cast the net on the right side of the ship, and ye shall find. They cast therefore, and now they were not able to draw it for the multitude of fishes. Therefore that disciple whom Jesus loved saith unto Peter, It is the Lord. Now when Simon Peter heard that it was the Lord, he girt his fisher's coat unto him, (for he was naked,) and did cast himself into the sea.**
>
> **— John 21:2-7**

Although the disciples weren't sure who was instructing them, they obeyed anyway — and caught so many fish that they weren't even able to pull their nets into the boat! Once they realized it was Jesus, they worked to get their nets in and make their way to the shore where the Lord was waiting with a roaring fire and a sampling of fish already cooking.

That same night, Jesus sat around a campfire with them, eating fish with them and spending time fellowshipping. John 21:14 says, "This is now the third time that Jesus shewed himself to his disciples, after that he was risen from the dead."

Jesus Appeared to More Than 500 People at One Time

After Jesus' resurrection, "…He shewed himself alive after his passion by many infallible proofs, being seen of them forty days, and speaking of the things pertaining to the kingdom of God" (Acts 1:3). Can you imagine! For 40 days, Jesus continued making various appearances all over the region, giving His followers indisputable proof that it was indeed Him and that He was fully alive.

During those 40 days, Jesus performed signs and wonders, taught about the Kingdom of God, and spent time with His disciples, eating with them, talking with them, walking with them, and even helping them catch a boatload of fish.

The apostle Paul wrote in his first letter to the believers at Corinth that at one time before Jesus returned to Heaven, He appeared to more than 500 people at one time:

> **And that he [Jesus] was seen of Cephas, then of the twelve: after that, he was seen of above five hundred brethren at once; of whom the greater part remain unto this present, but some are fallen asleep. After that, he was seen of James; then of all the apostles.**
> **— 1 Corinthians 15:5-7**

This passage is just extraordinary! It is understood that this letter was written around 55 AD, possibly during Paul's third missionary journey. Here Paul writes that the majority of the people who were among the 500 that Jesus appeared to all at once were still living to tell about it!

Jesus' Final Appearance to the Disciples in Galilee

Before ascending into Heaven, Jesus appeared to His disciples one last time as they gathered on the same mountain in Galilee where He had first ordained them. On this final occasion together, He gave them — and us — the Great Commission:

> **…All power is given unto me in heaven and in earth. Go ye therefore, and teach all nations, baptizing them in the name of the Father, and of the Son, and of the Holy Ghost: teaching them to observe all things whatsoever I have commanded you:**

and, lo, I am with you always, even unto the end of the world. Amen.

— Matthew 28:18-20

Friend, there were multiple eyewitness accounts that Jesus was raised from the dead. This is not a hoax, a myth, or a fabricated legend. Jesus really lived, He really died, and He really rose again!

In the next lesson, we'll see what Jesus has been doing for the last 2,000 years.

STUDY QUESTIONS

Study to shew thyself approved unto God, a workman that needeth not to be ashamed, rightly dividing the word of truth.
— 2 Timothy 2:15?

1. In Jesus' glorified condition, He was able to appear and disappear, to travel great distances, and to even supernaturally pass through solid walls and locked doors. According to God's Word, what is going to happen to *your physical body*, and what will it be like for all eternity? Check out Romans 8:29; 1 Corinthians 15:49-53; 1 John 3:2; and Philippians 3:21 for the answer.

2. The first time Jesus appeared to His disciples, Thomas was not with the group. According to John 20:24-29, how did Thomas respond to the disciples' report of seeing Jesus? What did Jesus lovingly do to strengthen Thomas' faith?

3. Has the Lord ever met you in a similar way — proving Himself to you like He did to Thomas at a time when you were struggling in your faith? If so, briefly share what happened.

PRACTICAL APPLICATION

But be ye doers of the word, and not hearers only, deceiving your own selves.
— James 1:22

1. Mary Magdalene was the first person to come face to face with Jesus in His resurrected form. In that extraordinary moment, Christ called Mary by name. Have you ever heard Jesus whisper your name? Have you ever heard Him tell you that He loves you or sensed His tender

affection and care? If so, how were you affected and how did you respond?

2. The morning of Jesus' resurrection, He appeared to two of His disciples, listening and talking with them. But they didn't recognize Him because they were very discouraged. Have you been there? Are you there now? Pause and pray: *"Lord, in what areas of my life am I blinded to Your presence?"* Be still and listen. What is the Holy Spirit showing you? Invite Him into those situations, receiving the wisdom, strength, and encouragement He provides.

LESSON 14

TOPIC

What Has Jesus Been Doing for the Last 2,000 Years?

SCRIPTURES

1. **Acts 1:3** — …He shewed himself alive after his passion by many infallible proofs, being seen of them forty days, and speaking of the things pertaining to the kingdom of God.

2. **Acts 1:9-11** — …He was taken up; and a cloud received him out of their sight. And while they looked stedfastly toward heaven as he went up, behold, two men stood by them in white apparel; which also said, Ye men of Galilee, why stand ye gazing up into heaven? this same Jesus, which is taken up from you into heaven, shall so come in like manner as ye have seen him go into heaven.

3. **Acts 3:21** — [Jesus] Whom the heaven must receive until the times of restitution of all things, which God hath spoken by the mouth of all his holy prophets since the world began.

4. **Acts 2:33** — Therefore being by the right hand of God exalted, and having received of the Father the promise of the Holy Ghost, he hath shed forth this, which ye now see and hear.

5. **Hebrews 8:6** — But now hath he obtained a more excellent ministry, by how much also he is the mediator of a better covenant, which was established upon better promises.

6. **Hebrews 7:24,25** — But this man, because he continueth ever, hath an unchangeable priesthood. Wherefore he is able also to save them to the uttermost that come unto God by him, seeing he ever liveth to make intercession for them.
7. **Hebrews 4:15,16** — For we have not an high priest which cannot be touched with the feeling of our infirmities; but was in all points tempted like as we are, yet without sin. Let us therefore come boldly unto the throne of grace, that we may obtain mercy, and find grace to help in time of need.

GREEK WORDS

1. "excellent" (*diaphoros*) — incomparable, unparalleled, unsurpassed, unmatched, finest, greatest, or most excellent
2. "boldly" (*parresia*) — freedom of speech; pictures a person who speaks his mind and who does it straightforwardly and with great confidence
3. "obtain" (*lambano*) — to seize or to lay hold of something in order to make it your very own; pictures reaching out to grab, to capture, or to take possession of something; it can either mean to violently lay hold of something to seize and take it as one's very own, or it can depict a person who gently and graciously receives something that is freely and easily given
4. "find" (*eurisko*) — a discovery made by searching; a discovery made as a result of an intense investigation, scientific study, or scholarly research
5. "help in time of need" (*boetheia*) — a word of military connotation that was first and foremost used to describe a moment when a soldier got into trouble and a fellow soldier was alerted to his dangerous situation; because the alerted soldier was committed to the soldier in trouble, he went to battle to defend his co-fighter and fight for his well-being, safety, and security; simply hearing that a fellow soldier was in need was enough to beckon the other soldier to battle and to motivate him to spare no effort in order to rescue and bring his fellow soldier to a place of safety and protection

SYNOPSIS

In our last lesson, we saw that after Jesus rose from the grave, He appeared multiple times to multiple people. He even ate with His disciples and allowed them to touch and examine His resurrected body so they could see and know for sure it was really Him.

For 40 days, "...He shewed himself alive after his passion by many infallible proofs..." (Acts 1:3). In fact, the apostle Paul recorded that on one occasion, Jesus showed Himself to more than 500 people at once! (*See* 1 Corinthians 15:6.) After those 40 days, He ascended into Heaven, which brings us to a very important question: *What has Jesus been doing for the last 2,000 years?*

The emphasis of this lesson:

After Jesus ascended into Heaven, He sent the Holy Spirit to indwell believers and took on the role as our Great High Priest. He wants to hear you boldly and candidly say what's on your heart. His mercy, grace, and help in time of need are available to you at any time. He is your Great Warrior who stands ready to swing into action and come to your rescue.

The Disciples Watched Jesus Ascend Into Heaven

The book of Acts was written by Luke, the beloved physician and historian. He began his record of the development and happenings of the Early Church by first talking about Jesus' final appearance to His closest followers. Specifically, Luke wrote:

> **...He [Jesus] shewed himself alive after his passion by many infallible proofs, being seen of them forty days, and speaking of the things pertaining to the kingdom of God.**
>
> **—Acts 1:3**

Jesus answered some last-minute questions from His disciples then urged them to "...not depart from Jerusalem, but wait for the promise of the Father..." (Acts 1:4). What happened next was remarkable:

> **...While they beheld, he was taken up; and a cloud received him out of their sight. And while they looked stedfastly toward heaven as he went up, behold, two men stood by them in white apparel; which also said, Ye men of Galilee, why stand ye gazing up into heaven? this same Jesus, which is taken up from you**

**into heaven, shall so come in like manner as ye have seen him
go into heaven.**

— Acts 1:9-11

Imagine that! One moment you are speaking with Jesus face to face, and the next minute He's ascending and accelerating upward and out of sight into the clouds! That's what happened to the disciples, and as they watched Him go, two angels suddenly appeared in "white apparel," which in Greek describes *garments that glisten and shine like lightning.*

Jesus' Return Will Be Similar to His Ascension at His Second Coming

The two angels who appeared at Jesus' departure declared that He will one day return to the earth in the same manner He left. Peter talked about this in the message he preached on the Day of Pentecost just a few days later. He said, "And he [God] shall send Jesus Christ…Whom the heaven must receive until the times of restitution of all things, which God hath spoken by the mouth of all his holy prophets since the world began" (Acts 3:20,21).

Only once every prophecy has finally been fulfilled and every soul that will be saved has been saved will Jesus return — and His *Second Coming* will take place in exactly the same way as His departure nearly 2,000 years ago. But at His Second Coming — which is after the Rapture of the Church — Jesus will not return as a humble Servant; He will be the mighty King of kings and the Lord of lords!

When the disciples watched Jesus ascend into a cloud of glory that received Him into Heaven, it was the last time Jesus was ever seen in His physical human form. Since that time, people have experienced supernatural moments when they've seen Jesus in visions and in dreams. Likewise, we know that Jesus is touching people's lives today through His Church, which Scripture even refers to as the *Body of Christ.*

Nevertheless, Jesus Himself — in His actual physical form — left the earth approximately 2,000 years ago, and He has been absent ever since and will only return in physical form when every scripture related to the last days has been fulfilled and when the last soul to be saved has been saved.

Jesus Now Serves in a 'More Excellent Ministry'

When Peter stood up and preached on the Day of Pentecost, one of the things he said was:

> **This Jesus hath God raised up, whereof we all are witnesses.**
>
> **Therefore being by the right hand of God exalted, and having received of the Father the promise of the Holy Ghost, he hath shed forth this, which ye now see and hear.**
>
> — **Acts 2:32,33**

Once Jesus completed His work on earth, He ascended into Heaven where He now sits at the Father's right hand. His first order of business was to pour out the gift of the Holy Spirit upon the Church, which is exactly what happened on the Day of Pentecost.

For the last 2,000 years, Jesus has been alive and well seated at the right hand of God the Father. During that time, His focus has shifted from being the Passover Lamb of God to serving as the Mediator between us and the Father. This truth is made quite plain in the book of Hebrews:

> **But now hath he obtained a more excellent ministry, by how much also he is the mediator of a better covenant, which was established upon better promises.**
>
> — **Hebrews 8:6**

The Bible says Jesus' present phase of ministry is "a more excellent ministry," and the word "excellent" in the original Greek language means *incomparable, unparalleled, unsurpassed, unmatched, finest, greatest,* or *most excellent.* This means Jesus' present-day ministry is not even to be compared to His previous earthly ministry.

So what is it about this present phase of Jesus' ministry that makes it more excellent? What is He doing as He is seated at the right hand of the Father that is so *incomparable, unparalleled, unsurpassed, unmatched, the finest, the greatest,* and *the most excellent of all?* The answer is: *Jesus has become our Great High Priest!*

Jesus Is Our Great High Priest

After Jesus' miraculous resurrection from the dead, the moment He sat down at the Father's right hand and everything was placed under His feet,

His ministry was initiated to be a Great High Priest to everyone who calls upon His name. Under the Old Covenant, there were many priests, but each of them eventually died due to their human condition.

That is not the case with Jesus. Hebrews 7:24 and 25 declares:

> But this man [Jesus], because he continueth ever, hath an unchangeable priesthood. Wherefore he is able also to save them to the uttermost that come unto God by him, seeing he ever liveth to make intercession for them.

This passage defines Christ's ministry today. His Priesthood has no end, and He is able to save each one of us who comes to God through Him. And Jesus lives forever to intercede or pray for us.

The writer of Hebrews also said:

> For we have not an high priest which cannot be touched with the feeling of our infirmities; but was in all points tempted like as we are, yet without sin. Let us therefore come boldly unto the throne of grace, that we may obtain mercy, and find grace to help in time of need.
> — Hebrews 4:15,16

Jesus has become your Great High Priest — He is your personal representative who sits at the right hand of the Father in Heaven. His ministry today is to represent you to the Father, and because Jesus lived on the earth as a Man, He experienced and understands every problem or temptation that will ever come your way.

The fact is, Jesus has faced every temptation that any human being will ever encounter in life. Therefore, anything you talk to Him about is something that He personally experienced in some way. As a human being, He was tempted in every way possible — yet **He did not sin**. Therefore, He is qualified today to sit at the Father's right hand and intercede on our behalf.

'Boldly' Come to God's Throne

Because of the finished work of Jesus Christ — through the sacrifice of His broken body and the shedding of His life's blood — we have access into the very presence of the Father (*see* Hebrews 10:19-22). Accordingly, the writer of Hebrews says:

Let us therefore come boldly unto the throne of grace, that we may obtain mercy, and find grace to help in time of need.
— Hebrews 4:16

Notice that word "boldly." In Greek, this describes *freedom of speech* and pictures *a person who speaks his mind and who does it straightforwardly with great confidence.* In the First Century, at the time the book of Hebrews was written, this word "boldly" depicted a frankness that was so bold, it could be met with resistance, hostility, and opposition.

Many thought it just wasn't acceptable to speak so candidly, so when someone spoke his mind and his thoughts this freely, his outspokenness would often be met with resistance and rebuke time and time again.

But that is not the case with God. He welcomes our candidness and great confidence, commanding us in Hebrews 4:16 to come "boldly" before His throne of grace. This means Jesus invites us to get straight to the point when we talk to Him!

He will never be turned off, offended, or insulted when you freely speak your heart and mind to Him. Likewise, you need never fear that you are too frank, too bold, too forthright, too honest, too outspoken, or too blunt when you open your heart to God about your needs and struggles or when you request His help.

Of course, this doesn't mean you should be disrespectful or irreverent — we should always have a healthy reverential fear of the Lord. But at the same time, you do not need to be afraid to speak exactly what is on your heart. Jesus wants to hear what you have to say to Him! That is what the Greek word for "boldly" means.

'Obtain' His Mercy

Looking again at Hebrews 4:16, we read, "Let us therefore come boldly unto the throne of grace, that we may obtain mercy, and find grace to help in time of need."

The word "obtain" here is important. It is a form of the Greek word *lambano*, and it means *to seize or to lay hold of something in order to make it your very own.* Hence, we could translate the first part of Hebrews 4:16 to say, "Let us come boldly to the throne of grace and speak freely with confidence, seizing and laying hold of mercy in order to make it our very own…."

Additionally, this word *lambano* — translated here as "obtain" — pictures *someone reaching out to grab, to capture*, or *to take possession of something*. This means there is mercy available to you from God that you can reach out and grab and take possession of.

Furthermore, this word *lambano* can also mean *to violently lay hold of something to seize and take it as one's very own*, or *it can depict a person who gently and graciously receives something that is freely and easily given*. There are times when it's easy for you to graciously receive God's mercy. But there are also moments when you're dealing with a lot of challenges, and you have to push through the barriers of your emotions, thoughts, and will in order to reach out and forcibly take hold of God's mercy by faith. That is a picture of what this word "obtain" *lambano* means.

Jesus is always there, waiting mercifully to help anyone who comes to Him by faith. He is ready and willing to give you exactly what you need. All you have to do is open your heart and receive it by faith. If you're ready to receive God's mercy, it is waiting for you in His presence.

'Find' God's Grace

Hebrews 4:16 also promises that you will "…find grace to help in time of need." The word "find" here is a form of the Greek word *eurisko*, which describes *a discovery made by searching* or *a discovery made as a result of an intense investigation, scientific study, or scholarly research*. It is interesting to note that the word "eureka," which means "I found it," is derived from the Greek word *eurisko*.

The use of this word *eurisko* means that sometimes you have to put your whole heart and soul into seeking what you need from God. And if you will pour all your effort and energy into searching for and discovering God's help, you will come to a "eureka" moment where you will find exactly what you need.

Imagine a researcher who, after working long hours and searching for a long time, suddenly finds what he has been seeking! In that unforgettable moment of joyful euphoria, he shrieks, "EUREKA!" — in other words: "I FOUND IT!"

Receive 'Help in Time of Need'

Something else that is very interesting about Hebrews 4:16 is the phrase "help in time of need." These words are a translation of a military term that first and foremost was used to describe a moment when a soldier got into trouble and a fellow soldier was alerted to his dangerous situation. And because the alerted soldier was committed to the soldier in trouble, he went to battle to defend his co-fighter and fight for his well-being, safety, and security.

Simply hearing that a fellow soldier was in need was enough to beckon the other soldier to battle and to motivate him to spare no effort in order to rescue and bring his fellow comrade to a place of safety and protection. All of that meaning is in the phrase "help in time of need."

Because this particular word is used in this text, we know that when we get into trouble and Jesus is alerted by our prayers, He swings into action to come to our defense! This is a vivid picture of real intercessory ministry.

Jesus is our Great Intercessor — our Great High Priest — and if we will go to Him and present our case, He will intercede for us and go to battle for us in our time of need. Indeed, He will rise up like a mighty warrior who is ready to go into battle to fight for us until we are delivered, freed, and brought into a place of safety!

That is the kind of "help" we will find if we present our needs to Jesus! It is a picture of protection, a rescue, or a remedy for whatever troubles us. To all who call out to Him in faith, Jesus provides protection and rescue to those who are in trouble. He is able to bring a remedy to whatever problem is ailing any person who boldly comes to Him in faith and asks for His assistance!

Jesus will help...

- Those who need healing for their bodies.
- Those who are bound and need deliverance.
- Those who are tormented and need peace.
- Those whose marriages and families are in trouble.
- Those who need provision or who need a financial breakthrough.
- Those who are in need in any area of their life.

Don't Fight Alone — Go to God's Throne!

Since all of this is true, and Jesus is our Great High Priest who is ever interceding for us — since He is our Great Warrior who stands ready to swing into action and come to our rescue — there is *no reason* for us to fight our battles on our own!

Why would we ever try to slug it out with the enemy on our own when the Greatest Warrior in the universe, the One who was raised from the dead and defeated death and the work of the devil, stands ready to swing into action and fight on our behalf?

Friend, if you've ever wondered what Jesus has been doing for the last 2,000 years, now you know. After He came to the earth, humbled Himself to the point of dying on the Cross, and was raised from the dead, He then ascended on high where He sat down at the Father's right hand and poured out the gift of the Holy Spirit upon the Church.

Today — RIGHT NOW — Jesus has His eyes fixed on you. He is seated at the right hand of the Father ever living to make intercession for you and for anyone who comes to Him by faith. He fights for every believer who comes boldly and honestly and who earnestly seeks His assistance. He will swing into action to lead you, guide you, and fight for you! By the strength of His Spirit, He will enable you to do whatever the will of God has planned for your life!

This is the "more excellent ministry" that has kept Jesus very busy for the past 2,000 years!

STUDY QUESTIONS

Study to shew thyself approved unto God, a workman that needeth not to be ashamed, rightly dividing the word of truth.
— 2 Timothy 2:15

1. The two angels who appeared just after Jesus' ascension into Heaven declared He will one day return to earth in the same manner He left (*see* Acts 1:10,11). This return to earth will be Jesus' *Second Coming*. What does the Bible say about this cataclysmic event in Matthew 24:30,31; 26:64; Zechariah 14:3-5; Jude 14,15; Revelation 1:7? How is the Second Coming different than the Rapture of the Church talked about in First Thessalonians 4:15-17 and First Corinthians 15:51,52?

2. Jesus extends a personal invitation for you to come to Him anytime, anywhere, about anything. Carefully reflect on His loving words to you in Matthew 11:28-30 (*AMPC*):

Come to Me, all you who labor and are heavy-laden and over-burdened, and I will cause you to rest. [I will ease and relieve and refresh your souls.] Take My yoke upon you and learn of Me, for I am gentle (meek) and humble (lowly) in heart, and you will find rest (relief and ease and refreshment and recreation and blessed quiet) for your souls. For My yoke is wholesome (useful, good—not harsh, hard, sharp, or pressing, but comfortable, gracious, and pleasant), and My burden is light and easy to be borne.

PRACTICAL APPLICATION

> But be ye doers of the word, and not hearers only,
> deceiving your own selves.
> —James 1:22

1. Jesus is your Great Intercessor and your Great Warrior. Just as a committed fellow soldier spares no effort to swing into action and bring his fellow comrade to a place of safety and protection, if you'll go to Jesus and present your case, He will intercede for you and go to battle for you in your time of need. How does hearing this biblical truth from Hebrews 4:16 encourage you? Consider these amazing promises from your Heavenly Father:

God's your Guardian, right at your side to protect you — shielding you from sunstroke, sheltering you from moonstroke. God guards you from every evil, he guards your very life. He guards you when you leave and when you return, he guards you now, he guards you always.
                                                     —Psalm 121:5-8 (*MSG*)

In the day when I called, You answered me; and You strengthened me with strength (might and inflexibility to temptation) in my inner self.
                                                     —Psalm 138:3 (*AMPC*)

For because He Himself [in His humanity] has suffered in being tempted (tested and tried), He is able [immediately] to run to the cry of (assist, relieve) those who are being tempted

and tested and tried [and who therefore are being exposed to suffering].

— Hebrews 2:18 (*AMPC*)

2. When it comes to your praying, God welcomes your candidness and great confidence. In Hebrews 4:16, He commands you to come "boldly" before His throne of grace. Knowing He will never be turned off, offended, or insulted when you freely speak your heart and mind, what will you finally talk to Him about? Take time now to honestly tell Him about what is weighing on you — your hurts, your habits, and your frustrations. Remember, His *mercy* and *grace* are available to you — and they are NEW every morning! (*See* Lamentations 3:22,23.)

LESSON 15

TOPIC

Copy Every Stroke of the Master and Walk in the Footprints of Jesus!

SCRIPTURES

1. **1 Peter 2:21** — For even hereunto were ye called: because Christ also suffered for us, leaving us an example, that ye should follow his steps.

GREEK WORDS

1. "suffered" (*pascho*) — to suffer; used to describe the passion or suffering that Jesus experienced in His last hours
2. "example" (*hupogrammos*) — pictures a school child who carefully watches his teacher write the letters of the alphabet and then painstakingly copies each letter, matching it as closely as possible to the original letters written by his teacher
3. "steps" (*ichnos*) — footprints

SYNOPSIS

Have you ever watched a little boy put on his father's shoes and try to walk in them? Or have you ever caught a glimpse of a little girl trying on her mom's high heels? These are classic examples of how children naturally attempt to imitate their parents.

This is what the apostle Paul had in mind when he instructed us to "…be imitators of God [copy Him and follow His example], as well-beloved children [imitate their father]" (Ephesians 5:1 *AMPC*). Jesus Christ was a visible example of our invisible Heavenly Father, and just as He imitated God, we are to copy His every stroke and walk in His footsteps.

The emphasis of this lesson:

Peter wrote specifically about how we're to respond to suffering, admonishing us to become excellent students of Jesus, our Master Teacher, copying His every action and following in His footsteps. He has gone before us and is our Chief Example and Mentor, showing us what we must do in each difficult situation we face.

Christ Left Us His Example

This is our fifteenth and final lesson, and from the time we began our journey, we have learned about Jesus' most trying moments during His final hours on the earth. We have also read about His intense agony in Gethsemane and seen His immense power on display on the night He was betrayed.

We covered His arrest and brutal abuse at the hands of the religious leaders and the temple police as well as the ridicule and mockery He suffered from Herod and the soldiers. Jesus then endured the horrific Roman scourge, a crown of thorns being thrust upon His head, and nails being driven into His hands and feet.

Through it all, "He did not retaliate when he was insulted, nor threaten revenge when he suffered. He left his case in the hands of God, who always judges fairly" (1 Peter 2:23 *NLT*).

Christ was crucified and buried and then raised back to life on the third day. He now lives forevermore as our Great High Priest, representing us before the Father and interceding on our behalf. He invites us to boldly come to Him in prayer about everything and anything, believing He will swing into action as our Mighty Warrior to defend us and put us back on our feet when we need help.

Peter Wrote Specifically About
How We're To Respond to Suffering

When we face challenging issues that arise in our life, we must learn how to imitate Jesus and commit ourselves and our situations into the hands of the Father who sees all things and judges everything fairly.

In the First Century, many believers were suffering a great deal of unfair treatment because of their faith, especially at the hands of the Roman government. That is what was happening to the Christians Peter was writing to, and in his first letter he told them:

> **For even hereunto were ye called: because Christ also suffered for us, leaving us an example, that ye should follow in his steps.**
> **— 1 Peter 2:21**

Keep in mind, these believers were suffering unjustly for their faith in Christ, and they had no legal recourse with which to defend themselves. Yet God's Word commanded them to respect, submit to, and pray for the very government that was harassing and killing them.

Notice the word "suffered" in First Peter 2:21. In Greek, it means *to suffer*, but here, this word is used to specifically describe *the passion or suffering that Jesus experienced in His last hours.* There are many instances in the New Testament where this Greek word for "suffered" is used, all of which carry the idea of *suffering, undergoing hardship, being ill-treated,* or *experiencing adversity.*

Jesus not only suffered an onslaught of brutality in His final hours, but also a plethora of unpleasurable experiences throughout His entire life. When He was a child, His family suffered as they fled from the murderous plots of King Herod the Great. During His ministry, Jesus suffered at the hands of religious leaders who hated Him and continually leveled false accusations against Him.

He also had to constantly put up with the immature behavior of His disciples as He loved them, taught them, and set an example for them. Even worse, Jesus suffered betrayal at the hands of Judas Iscariot who was one of His closest associates.

Scripture says that in the Garden of Gethsemane, the mental and emotional turmoil Jesus endured was so intense that His sweat was as great drops of blood falling down to the ground. And in the end, Jesus suffered the barbaric Roman scourge and was then crucified and died a most horrific death on the Cross.

Yet through all these different levels of suffering, Jesus lived above the fray and loved those who treated Him unjustly.

We Must Become Students
Who Follow the Example of Our Teacher

Again, at the time Peter was writing his epistle, the people he was addressing needed to know how to respond to unjust situations that they could not change and in which they had no legal recourse. To them and to us, Peter said, "…Christ also suffered for us, leaving us an example, that ye should follow in his steps" (1 Peter 2:21).

The word "example" in Greek pictures a school child who carefully watches his teacher write the letters of the alphabet. The student then painstakingly copies each letter, matching it as closely as possible to the original letters written by his teacher.

Can you remember when you were in school and first learning to write the letters of the alphabet? Rick took us back to his earliest memories in his first-grade classroom when he was learning to write his letters.

After carefully studying how his teacher wrote every letter of the alphabet on the blackboard, Rick would take his pencil in hand and begin to copy what she'd written in his notebook. With all his might, he'd press down with his pencil onto the paper to write those letters, and he pushed so hard that he formed a callous on his finger that he still has to this day. It is a permanent reminder that he gave 100 percent of his concentration to exactly duplicating every letter his teacher had written.

Day after day, he wrote those letters over and over again, filling his tablet with pages of writing until he finally mastered each letter of the alphabet. It took concentration and commitment, but in time he learned to write those letters exactly as his teacher had shown him.

This is a vivid picture of what the word "example" in First Peter 2:21 means. When Peter wrote this verse, that is the image he had in mind when he said, "…Christ also suffered for us, leaving us an *example*, that ye should follow in his steps" (1 Peter 2:21). When we are in a difficult situation, we are to painstakingly follow Jesus' example, copying every stroke of the Master. Christ is our Master Teacher, and His Word is like the spiritual "blackboard" that we must learn to focus on so that we can replicate His example in our own lives.

Things We Must Learn

We must go to the gospels and begin to read those pages with the heart of a student who studies and endeavors to copy every stroke of his teacher's pen. As we study Christ's example in the Scriptures, we will learn...

- How Jesus dealt with unfair criticism — so we can respond like Him when we are unfairly criticized.

- How Jesus responded to attacks that were waged against Him — so we can know how to respond in His strength to attacks that come against each of us.

- How Jesus responded to people when they failed or betrayed Him — so we can respond the same way when people disappoint or hurt us.

- How Jesus carried Himself with grace and dignity even in the midst of unspeakable abuse — so we can then draw on His strength to walk through difficult situations with the same grace and dignity.

- How He forgave His accusers every step of the way — so we can forgive those who mistreat or malign us.

The truth is, sometimes we really do face unpleasant situations in which we may feel mistreated, abused, or discriminated against. As long as we live in a world where evil exists, where the devil operates, and where unsaved people have their way, evil and injustice will touch our lives from time to time.

So when you find yourself in a situation that seems unfair and unjust, you must learn to ask yourself, *How did Jesus respond in such a situation, and how does God expect me to respond?* Then, perhaps in a deeper way than you've ever done before, invite Jesus to walk with you through your journey, guiding you by His Spirit through each difficulty and challenge that arises along the way.

Examples of Mistreatment

In any given situation, we must do everything possible to resolve conflicts with friends, family, coworkers, and fellow Christians, protecting ourselves and our reputation spiritually and legally. Yet sometimes things happen that are beyond our control, are not so easily resolved, and for which there is no easy recourse. For example…

What are you to do if your employer treats you badly? If for no obvious reason your boss mistreats you, and the situation goes on for a long time, how should you respond? You could go find another job, but a similar situation could be replicated again. How should you respond to the foul treatment you are receiving from your superiors?

How about the difficulties with fellow employees? What are you to do if they hurt you, try to undercut you, or attempt to get you demoted or fired? What course of action should you take? Perhaps you've taken steps to befriend them, but nothing seems to improve the situation. How should you respond to the unfair treatment you're experiencing?

Maybe you're a student who feels persecuted by fellow students. These are classmates who don't share your faith in Christ and who dislike your personal convictions. You know you can't quit school in reaction to this difficult situation. But exactly how does God expect you to respond?

Perhaps your family members are hostile toward you and treat you poorly. Maybe because they don't understand your faith or agree with the direction you're taking in life, they tend to belittle you, mock you, or ignore and ostracize you. This is especially difficult when you know the Holy Spirit is the One leading you to take a particular course of action. Clearly, you can't swap your family for another one, so how should you respond?

Whenever we are feeling maligned and mistreated, it's a prime opportunity for the devil to tempt us to become bitter, angry, hard-hearted, and resentful of those who have treated us unjustly. But our wrong response won't do enough to improve our situation. It may temporarily alleviate the pressure put on our ego or bring about a short-lived change in scenery. But ultimately, it will only produce negative consequences in the long run. That's why we must absolutely refuse to allow the devil to sow into our heart those negative emotions that bear only bad fruit.

In all of the above examples of mistreatment, we need to look at the "blackboard," which is God's Word, and see how our Master Teacher responded when He was in similar circumstances. Combing through the gospels and studying the life of Christ and then copying every stroke of the Master is the key. Just as we replicated the letters of our schoolteacher on paper, we are to keep practicing Christ's behavior until it is replicated in our life.

Follow in Jesus' 'Steps'

Looking once more at First Peter 2:21, we read, "For even hereunto were ye called: because Christ also suffered for us, leaving us an example, that ye should follow his steps." The Greek word for "steps" at the end of this verse is actually the word *footprints*. Hence, as we study and see how Jesus handled suffering, we are to follow in His *footsteps*.

Rick shared how when his sons were little and they were traveling and doing ministry, they would often stop and walk on the beach together. After removing their shoes, Rick would make footprints in the sand and challenge the boys to do their best to follow in his steps. Sometimes his footprints were close together, and other times he spread them far apart.

After wandering this way and that, making several pathways along the shore, Rick would turn around to see how his little ones were doing. Usually, one or two of them would be carefully trying to place their little feet neatly into his giant footsteps and follow in them. At the same time, at least one of the boys could be seen leaping from one footprint to the next. This is a picture of what Peter instructed us to do in First Peter 2:21.

When we find that we are in a difficult place, it is time to follow in the footsteps of Jesus. He has gone before us, leaving His footprints to show us what we must do in each situation. Rather than try to figure it all out by ourselves, we can just focus on Jesus and step exactly into His same steps.

Christ has given us a pattern to follow, and if we will step in His footsteps rather than just make our own path, we will do what is right in each circumstance. Sometimes it will be relatively easy, but other times it will require a huge leap of faith on our part.

The Answers You Need
Are Found in the Life of Jesus

Perhaps you've been praying for guidance, trying to understand how to deal with the conflicts you've encountered. Now you know that the answers you need are found in the life of Jesus. He is your Chief Example, your Teacher, your Mentor — the One you are called to copy and to follow.

So in addition to praying for wisdom and guidance, you must open your Bible to read from all four gospels to see what Jesus did in the same type of unjust and unfair situations you are facing. You are to learn from the Master and walk through your situation in the same manner that Jesus walked through His own challenges in this world.

Never forget that in Jesus' final hours...

- He was betrayed by one of His own disciples.
- Religious leaders spat on Him and beat Him with their fists.
- Soldiers slapped Him, mocked Him, and blasphemed Him.
- The crowd laughed at Him and rejected Him.
- Pilate ordered Him to be scourged and crucified, even though he knew Jesus was innocent.

Through it all, Jesus continued to walk in love — forgiving each of His offenders — and He is our example to show us how we should respond when we face injustice or find ourselves in difficult circumstances beyond our control.

Are you facing difficult times?

Are you being accused of things you didn't do or blamed for things of which you have no knowledge? Are you being mistreated or discriminated against? If your answer is "yes" to either of these questions, it is time for you to turn your eyes to the blackboard — God's Word — to study each stroke of the Master.

Once you see what He did and how He responded in situations similar to yours, it is your job to copy Him to the best of your ability. Rather than try to walk out your own path, put your feet in the footprints of Jesus. If you'll take this approach to the distressing challenges you're facing, the Holy

Spirit will empower you, and you'll be able to respond to every situation the way Jesus did.

You can't do this on your own, but Jesus didn't leave you to face life's challenges alone and without help. He sent the Holy Spirit as your Teacher and Guide to empower you so you can walk as Jesus walked in every situation you will ever face.

You probably won't get it exactly right the first or second time, but like a student who is learning to write, you must be determined to try and try again until you have finally mastered each stroke and learned to successfully respond to difficult situations as Jesus did when He walked the earth.

STUDY QUESTIONS

**Study to shew thyself approved unto God, a workman that needeth not to be ashamed, rightly dividing the word of truth.
— 2 Timothy 2:15**

1. As you complete this series on the death, burial, and resurrection of Jesus, what is one of your greatest takeaways? What scripture(s) and biblical principle(s) really impacted you that you want to remember?

2. The Bible serves as our "blackboard," containing the lessons we need in order to learn, grow, and make the most of this life. To understand the value and power of God's Word, read these verses:

    • Psalm 119:105,130

    • Acts 20:32

    • Romans 1:16

    • Romans 15:4

    • 1 Corinthians 10:11,12

    • 2 Timothy 3:15-17

    • Hebrews 4:12

    • James 1:21-25

    • 1 Peter 2:2

    What is the Holy Spirit showing you in these extraordinary passages?

PRACTICAL APPLICATION

> But be ye doers of the word, and not hearers only,
> deceiving your own selves.
> — James 1:22

1. Are you experiencing mistreatment? Is it with your boss or supervisor, your co-workers, your ministry leaders, or your family members? If you are, briefly describe what you are walking through. Then take the situation to the Lord in prayer, telling Him exactly how you feel and asking Him for the supernatural wisdom to know what to do. God promises to direct you and give you wisdom! (*See* Psalm 25:9,12; 32:8; 48:14; Isaiah 30:21; James 1:5; 3:17.)

2. In your own strength and ability, you cannot respond like Jesus. But Jesus didn't leave you to face the challenges of life alone and without help. He sent the Holy Spirit as your Teacher and Guide to empower you to copy His actions and follow in His footsteps. The same Spirit that raised Christ from the dead lives in *you*! (*See* Romans 8:11.) Second Corinthians 3:16-18 and Ephesians 3:16-21 talk about the Spirit's work in you. What is the Lord showing you in these verses? Take a few moments to pray, inviting the Holy Spirit to release His power in *every* area of your life — including the areas you may have previously kept off limits to Him.

3. Jesus, through the power of His Spirit, wants to walk with you through everything — even the difficulties you face (*see* Isaiah 43:1,2; 54:10; Hebrews 13:5,6). Draw strength from His Spirit (*see* Isaiah 41:10; Micah 3:8; Zechariah 4:6; 2 Corinthians 9:8; Philippians 4:13; James 4:6.) And commit to memory Habakkuk's declaration:

The Lord God is my Strength, my personal bravery, and my invincible army; He makes my feet like hinds' feet and will make me to walk [not to stand still in terror, but to walk] and make [spiritual] progress upon my high places [of trouble, suffering, or responsibility]!

— Habakkuk 3:19 (*AMPC*)

A Prayer To Receive Salvation

If you've never received Jesus as your Savior and Lord, now is the time for you to experience the new life Jesus wants to give you! To receive God's gift of salvation that can be obtained through Jesus alone, pray this prayer from your heart:

Jesus, I repent of my sin and receive You as my Savior and Lord. Wash away my sin with Your precious blood and make me completely new. I thank You that my sin is removed, and Satan no longer has any right to lay claim on me. Through Your empowering grace, I faithfully promise that I will serve You as my Lord for the rest of my life.

If you just prayed this prayer of salvation, you are born again! You are a brand-new creation in Christ! Would you please let us know of your decision by going to **renner.org/salvation**? We would love to connect with you and pray for you as you begin your new life in Christ.

Scriptures for further study: John 3:16; John 14:6; Acts 4:12; Ephesians 1:7; Hebrews 10:19,20; 1 Peter 1:18,19; Romans 10:9,10; Colossians 1:13; 2 Corinthians 5:17; Romans 6:4; 1 Peter 1:3

CLAIM YOUR FREE RESOURCE!

As a way of introducing you further to the teaching ministry of Rick Renner, we would like to send you FREE of charge his teaching, "How To Receive a Miraculous Touch From God" on CD or as an MP3 download.

In His earthly ministry, Jesus commonly healed *all* who were sick of *all* their diseases. In this profound message, learn about the manifold dimensions of Christ's wisdom, goodness, power, and love toward all humanity who came to Him in faith with their needs.

☑ **YES, I want to receive Rick Renner's monthly teaching letter!**

Simply scan the QR code to claim this resource or go to:
renner.org/claim-your-free-offer

Connect

WITH US!

www.ingramcontent.com/pod-product-compliance
Lightning Source LLC
Chambersburg PA
CBHW071441090426
42737CB00011B/1742